Adobe

Doorways

DOROTHY L. PILLSBURY

Vignettes by
M. J. Davis

THE LIGHTNING TREE
JENE LYON, PUBLISHER
SANTA FÉ, NEW MEXICO   U.S.A.

BY DOROTHY L. PILLSBURY

No High Adobe
Adobe Doorways
Roots In Adobe
Star Over Adobe

Library of Congress Catalog Card No. 52-11521

ISBN: 0-89016-070-8 (PA)   ISBN: 0-89016-076-7 (CL)

MANUFACTURED IN THE UNITED STATES OF AMERICA

Second Lightning Tree Edition—1986

THE LIGHTNING TREE   *Jene Lyon, Publisher*
P.O. Box 1837   Santa Fé, New Mexico 87504-1837   U.S.A.

Table of Contents

Little
Adobe Houses

ONE THING
the three peoples who live in northern New
Mexico have in common is a great contentment
with their squat adobe houses. Most of the
Pueblo Indians live in such houses and so do the
Spanish-Americans. Among the Anglos, a veri-
table cult of adobe dwellers has sprung up.

Tomes have been written about the adobe
houses of Santa Fe and vicinity. They go expertly into brickmaking, floor plans, *vigas, canales, portales,* and corner *fogones.* They delve
back into history and jump to modern architec-
tural approval. But the cult of adobe lovers
knows it is all surface stuff. It is like describing
a lovely and beguiling woman by giving her
dress size and naming her brand of cosmetics.

The cult knows that, in all the world, there
is nothing so heart-and-eye satisfying as a little

adobe house. They think of peach and apple blossoms stenciled pinkly against thick brown walls, of summer hollyhocks, crimson, yellow, and cream, reaching for flat roof-tops. They think something should be said about the silver bubbles of piñón smoke that float from stubby chimneys against autumn skies and fill the air with that fragrance which will be forever our New Mexico. Especially they want mentioned the little golden cubes of houses scattered like children's building blocks over the bleak whiteness of a winter's night.

The most ardent of the cult are converts with all the convert's zeal and fire. The natives, Indians and Spanish-American, take adobe all in stride as they take the russet-hued *tierra* and the rhythm of the seasons. It is the Anglo convert to adobe who has made of adobe-dwelling a philosophy and a song.

All Anglos who live in adobe houses are not members of the cult. Some live in them as they would live in any other kind of house and lament the drafts that filter in under poorly-hung doors and around out-of-plumb windows. They even use harsh words when they find one end of a room to be eighteen inches narrower than the other.

But real members of the cult drift to adobe living as naturally as tumbleweeds roll to a fence corner. It is a mistake to think they are all artists and writers. Some are clerks, schoolteachers, businessmen, bankers, lawyers, and plumbers. From time to time, some backslide, sell out, and depart for what they call civilized living. Back they come wild-eyed and breathless to buy raveling walls and sagging roof in the hope of resurrecting the dear lost love.

Visitors passing briefly through the country often become converts. "I'll never be happy until I own one of those little adobe houses," they exclaim. Nobody knows how many sales managers, stenographers, social workers, and steam fitters scattered through the length and breadth of the land are living with the memory of a little corner fireplace as a pillar of fire in the wilderness.

Members of the cult may be recognized by the fact that they always refer to their adobe houses as to living personalities. Also at some time or another, they ask wistfully, "What is there about a little adobe house?" Voices trail off vaguely into space. The question is never answered.

Mary Austin, who was a member of the

cult, knew. In her *Land of Journey's Ending*, she says that one really knows an adobe house "only when the mud roofs are muffled in snow and the flames of cedar run up the walls of corner fireplaces." But, alas, Mary did not explain much more about her little adobe house.

She, who loved this region with a passion, must have known that the primal charm of an adobe house is its earthiness. It does not have to be coaxed to blend with the soil. It is the soil. Brown adobe walls are the strong, warm arms of Earth-Mother around her children. Adobe dwellers recognize this vaguely. "I feel so secure," they say.

Other house walls merely shut out wind and cold. Adobe walls, often being out-of-line around openings, do not shut out the elements as effectually as those of other construction. But —and this is the essence of adobe—they give the effect of shutting out not only wind and cold, but the tumult of the world. That sense of security may well have come down a long psychological ladder from those faraway days when prehistoric man found his first real shelter in a clay-walled cave.

Next to earthliness, the adobe house beguiles with simplicity. As life becomes more and more involved, snarled and confused, an adobe house becomes an island of sanity in a sea of jitters. There is something about its sun-burnished outer walls and its plain, white inner spaces that says, "Why complicate living?" That simplicity has the magic ability to absorb the electrical and mechanical gadgets of modern living and still give the effect of the primitive.

Perhaps this magic ability to absorb the mechanics of modern living is part and parcel of nature's protective coloring. In spite of thick walls, an adobe house has no sharply defined line between indoors and out. It is as if the landscape obligingly moves inside. Perhaps it is because those walls are only a little elevation of the soil outside. Perhaps it is because the *vigas* —those cinnamon-colored shafts of pine trees which hold up the low ceiling—carry the memory of forest spaces down their lengths.

And then there is the *fogón,* that minute fireplace built across the corner of a room. It is whitely-kalsomined like the walls and its opening is beehive-shaped. Indented shelves where blue candles burn in tin candlesticks make it a kind of earthy altar where a strand of scarlet chiles and five ears of Indian corn pay tribute to the earth.

To sit around that tiny fireplace is to know that it is like no other fireplace on earth, be it red brick, white marble, or imported tile. To watch piñón logs fluttering sequined butterfly wings up its sooty inner sides, is to know why this small *fogón* is different from all others. That fire, burning without andirons, is mankind's old friend, the campfire. Around it have sat, from time's beginning, all of life's wanderers.

Such houses are not acquired merely by consultations with architects and contractors, nor by the signing of a check. The adobe houses of cult members evolve much as a sea shell adds a new cell or the wild plum tree sends a lace-draped branch toward the sun.

These adobe dwellers think someone, even in the midst of brick counting and plumbing specifications, should mention the deep accord that exists between their little mud houses and the natural universe about them. Moonlight gilds their walls at night, stars stare primly over the rounded edges of flat roofs. From the first froth of wild plum blossom to the time of snows when dark tufts of piñón trees tie white hillsides together, little adobe houses hum with deep contentment. It is a simple, humble little song, the merest thread of a melody caught from a deeper rhythm. But we who live in such little houses find our own hearts singing with them.

Gadgets Overtake the Bodgets

FOR FORTY YEARS Mr. and Mrs. Bodget had dreamed of the land where you have time to do all the things you've wanted to do. In Mr. Bodget's case that meant art. To Mrs. Bodget it meant wood carving and weaving. To both of them it meant humdrum living reduced to its utmost simplicity. Especially—I quote Mr. Bodget—it meant a retreat from the slavery of "modern gadgets."

During the forty years they had sampled the things they had wanted to do in tantalizing moments stolen from life in a city apartment. Mr. Bodget's life had consisted largely of tabulations, totalings, and sales graphs. Only occasionally could he manage a night-school course in art or visit a local gallery.

Mrs. Bodget's life had been even more complicated, rearing children and grandchildren in the cramped quarters of an apartment. Only at odd moments could she so much as hook a rug after a design of her own devising.

At last, thanks to a small bequest and an annuity they had built up, dollar by dollar, the Bodgets were able to move into the land of their dreams. On a northern New Mexico hilltop twenty miles from the nearest town, they found a small, crumbling adobe house and a three-hundred-mile view.

They had escaped! Here they could reduce the mechanics of living to the most simple requirements. Mr. Bodget could devote endless days to his painting. Mrs. Bodget could wood-carve and weave from morning to night.

Naturally, Mr. Bodget felt he should have some kind of studio for his activities in art. Consequently, their first year on the hilltop was given to converting one room of their small house into a studio and to building shelves and closets where none had ever been.

From Remedio Griego, a Spanish-American neighbor, the Bodgets soon mastered the simple craft of making adobe bricks from the red soil of their hilltop and of laying them in thick adobe walls. Soon the Bodgets were knee-deep in adobe. There was something alive about such building, the Bodgets thought. Adobe flowed.

It flowed all over the hilltop. The second year they built a garage for their battered car to save it from the variable elements of the region. Garden walls followed the garage. Terraces for fruit trees and an ever-expanding garden followed the terraces. Each year the Bodgets told each other that they would be settled down to their respective arts come another spring.

But the next year Mrs. Bodget felt she needed a workroom for her loom and wood-carving bench. That with more terraces, more fruit trees, more garden walls, more hollyhocks and Swiss chard, and a storage place for the canned produce therefrom took up another year.

By this time Mr. Bodget had mellowed enough in sun and wind to relent a trifle in respect to his original distaste for modern gadgets. Due to begrimed overalls and workshirts, he purchased the largest and latest washing machine he could find. It was so large that the only place he could find to put it was in his studio. Happily, the Bodgets took the rest of the year to build suitable housing for the washing machine.

So in sun and adobe the years rolled by. Mr. Bodget found the paint in his tubes drying up. Mrs. Bodget had not so much as threaded her loom. In between adobe building, planting, and terracing, the Bodgets just sat in deep content. Sometimes in the evening while their new self-changing record player gave them a musical background, Mr. Bodget read what the artists in Santa Fe and Taos were doing. He yawned pleasantly as he read. Mrs. Bodget hooked a rug.

In no time at all, seven years passed over the Bodget hilltop. It was a lovely place, open to sunsets and stars and the white cloud galleons of the sky. Fruit trees bloomed pink and silver against adobe walls. Mrs. Bodget's hollyhocks were the tallest in the region. Mr. Bodget's Swiss chard took first prize at the county fair.

One autumn night Mr. Bodget was stricken with regret. "Seven years," he sighed, "and not a picture painted." Mrs. Bodget extracted a much-read clipping from its place under the clock.

"Art and life are one," she read, "and the greatest of the arts is the art of living."

The Bodgets smiled knowingly at each other and went out on an upper terrace to watch the moon come up over their three-hundred-mile view.

The Grand Repast

WHEN Mrs. Apodaca's limited English and my much more limited Spanish break down in our conversations, we bridge the gap with pantomime that is far more dramatic than the almost forgotten Indian sign language. The results are often hilarious.

For reasons that are important only to myself, I have never been able to enjoy eating game. This is often embarrassing in a region that abounds with wild life and with nimrods who wish to present their friends with the evidence of their skill and hardihood.

But during the meatless weeks of the War, I broke down and accepted a huge saddle of venison. It was dressed and ready for the oven. It looked like any other roast from the meat market.

Day by day that venison roast froze harder and harder in my ice box, until I was forced to face the fact that I could never cook it, let alone eat it. Why not give it to my neighbor, Mrs. Apodaca, I reasoned. The people of Tenorio Flat, even in abundant times, know little meat. They use it thriftily for seasoning long-simmered sauces. They extend it endlessly, mixed with corn meal and rice. A slice of roast is almost unknown. With all the family Mrs. Apodaca has to cook for, and with the constant stream of big-hatted mealtime visitants from mountain villages, that great roast of venison would be a wonder and a boon.

"When I unwrapped the enormous roast in Mrs. Apodaca's small kitchen, she received it with delight. "It is not beef," she questioned, sniffing and prodding. "It is not sheep. What kind of *carne*—meat—is it, Señora?"

"Deer," I told her, somewhat apologetically, thinking of my own dislike.

"Dear," agreed Mrs. Apodaca instantly. "*Sí*, Señora, the *carne* takes the gold of kings to buy these days."

"No, no," I brushed aside the mercenary trend the conversation was taking. "No, not money—deer, deer, *el animalito!*"

Mrs. Apodaca shook her black-shawled head and looked blank. I could not think of the Spanish word for deer. But quickly I went into pantomime. I placed the thumbs of each hand above my eyebrows and spread my fingers to simulate antlers. So carried away was I with the performance, that I even extended the lower portion of my face in what I hoped looked like a deer's muzzle and stuck out the tip of my tongue as deer do when they nibble bushes. I was quite pleased with my act.

Mrs. Apodaca caught on instantly. "Ah, *venado*—deer—" she exclaimed and put her own thumbs to her head and spread her brown fingers to simulate antlers. She even went me one better, hopping stiff-legged about the room and sniffing the breeze in deer-like caution.

For days thereafter, over my somewhat monotonous omelet and salad, I pictured the Apodaca family sitting around the long, oilcloth-covered table in the fragrant little kitchen, enjoying an abundance of meat for the first time. Wood wagons filled with broad-hatted relatives from Chimayó and Córdova drove up just at mealtime. Evidently the news had spread.

And then Carmencita, my neighbor's long-legged daughter, appeared early one morning to say I was to prepare no dinner that night. My dinner was to be sent over on a tray by *mamacita*. With great anticipation I pictured Mrs. Apodaca's mounds of good red beans and her piles of blue corn tortillas.

Something momentous was in the wind. Men in blue jeans and sheepskin coats stopped to congratulate me on the *comida grande*—the grand repast—I was about to receive. Old ladies waved gayly at me through the window and smacked their lips. Even the *muchachos* marched through the yard, chanting, *"la comida grande, la comida grande."*

At candlelighting time, Mrs. Apodaca appeared with a large tray filled with brown pottery bowls. Behind her came Carmencita with another tray and more bowls. As lids were lifted from bowls, the most delectable odors filled the room. "I hope you like," Mrs. Apodaca said modestly. "Here are

> *Tamales, tacos, sopaipillas,*
> *Enchiladas, tortillas, empanadillas."*

It was like an anthem, and there was enough food to last me a week. Impetuously I called two friends to break all speed records to the Little Adobe House. The table, spread with an apricot-colored cloth, stood waiting for them in front of the corner fireplace. Candlelight twinkled on cherry-colored china. The brown bowls disclosed one hot savory surprise after the other. There was a mound of mashed brown beans from whose summit trickled rivulets of melted cheese. There were stacks of blue corn tortillas and piles of small crisp fritters as light as cottonwood fluff. There were *tamales* and *enchiladas* and bowls of fragrant sauces, red with tomato and *picante* with pounded chile to go with them. Little fried pies of apricot conserve sprinkled with piñón nuts ended the delectable meal. We consumed every crumb.

When I took all the brown bowls back to Mrs. Apodaca, I tried to tell her what pleasure she had given my guests and me. "It was superb," I said, "a masterpiece of New Mexican cookery."

Mrs. Apodaca smiled benignly. "It was good, no? I thought it would be good. Never, Señora, do I have so much *carne* to make it good. *Verdad!*"

To my horror, Mrs. Apodaca put two brown thumbs to her head and spread her fingers to simulate antlers. I left her hopping stiff-legged about her small, fragrant kitchen.

Home-Keeping Hearts

NOVEMBER
is the time of year when Santa Fe relaxes, like
a satisfied host whose approving guests have
departed. All through the spring, summer,
and early autumn months, we have shared our
homes, our old town and our spectacular countryside with tide after tide of visitors. It has
been a glorious time, for we have seen our region through new eyes. Remote Spanish villages,
Indian dances, hundreds of miles of uninhabited
space have become new to us, seen through the
eyes of our guests.

Now we can settle down and enjoy our old
town and our adobe *casitas*. Other adobe dwellers, whom we have not seen for months, spend
long evenings around the corner fireplace. We
do not talk much. We just stretch out our
grubby shoes to the piñón blaze and beam at

one another. Even the Little Adobe House takes on a new loveliness. One thing we are all agreed upon. We will stay at home. Little Spanish villages, Indian dances, and mesa tops will not see us for months and months. We will get back to our work. We will paint, carve wood, write poetry at regular hours.

The old town agrees. It yawns and smiles after a strenuous summer. Like ourselves, it is no longer on parade. Dry leaves fill adobe yards and vagabond tumbleweeds pile up in fence corners. The air is so clear and still, that at night we can hear the Diesel engines of transcontinental trains as they race through faraway hills. Let other people roam, we think, as we turn a page in a book we've been wanting to read for months.

When we wander down to the Plaza for the mail, it is good to see our narrow, crooked streets calm and orderly again. Not one car with a Texas license is dashing down one-way San Francisco Street from the wrong direction. Not one car from California is parked in the entrance to the fire station.

Going into the stores is almost like going home. Clerks greet us like long-lost friends. Mrs. Apodaca's *prima*—cousin, Lupita Salazar, is yawning behind her counter in a chain store

I frequent. "I need a gimlet, Lupita," I suggest in the midst of endless greeting.

"Jimlet, what is that?" inquires Lupita, startled out of the amenities.

"A little instrument to make holes for screws," I instruct.

Lupita shakes her head sadly. "We do not have a jimlet." To make sure, she leisurely visits all the other counters in the place, including the ribbon and notion counters. "Alas," she grieves on return from her tour of inspection, "we do not have a jimlet."

I go on down the street. It does not seem important wnether I have a gimlet or not. After awhile I hear the flurry of running feet behind me. It is Lupita, breathless, but waving a small object toward me. "I just left my counter and went across the street to another store. Here is your jimlet. Thirty-nine cents plus tax, Señora. *Por nada, por nada.*" Truly Santa Fe is itself again.

Looking in the bookstore window, I spy a friend I haven't seen all summer. With the same delightful sense of leisure I feel, she is examining a window full of books. We go arm in arm to fortify ourselves against the cold with a bowl of steaming soup. "Wonderful to be at home again," we both comment between mouthfuls. "No more galavanting till next spring."

"You've forgotten the Harvest Dance at Jémez Pueblo," my friend reproaches. "We haven't missed it for years and years." I think of lovely Jémez, with its high, pink cliffs and blue, blue mountain behind the cliffs. I think of pounding drums and feet that dance all day. "Of course we can't miss it," I agree.

Ten minutes later I meet another friend. We have a cup of hot chocolate together. "Wonderful to be at home again," we agree between sips. "No more gadding around the country."

"We never have seen a Guadalupe Day procession," my friend complains. "Let's scout around on the other side of the mountains over toward Mora. We might run into something good."

I agree to go to Mora. Half an hour later I meet another friend. "How about a bowl—?" I shake my head and we compromise on a bag of piñón nuts which we munch, not too expertly, on a seat in the plaza. "Wonderful to be at home again," we comment in unison. "No more wandering here and there over the country."

"How about the Matachines Dance? Remember last year?" I do remember Indians giving a dance that was partly Spanish with Moorish accents, and partly Indian. I remember how they blew down the wintry dance plaza in their strange oriental robes and headdresses to the rhythm of a violin and guitar instead of resounding *tombés*. Like bubbles of light they floated before the wind. "What kind of sandwiches shall I take?" I asked.

I go home by a roundabout route. I start a fire in the little fireplace and pick up that book I've been wanting to read for months. The telephone rings once or twice. One friend thinks we should go up in the Chama country and another "just to the edge of Navaho Land." I accept with exuberance. I close the unread book at page one. Almost apologetically, I glance at the Little Adobe House. Then I realize that the little house is endearing, because it is constantly being filled and refilled with the memory of beauty I bring it from all over the region.

Language of the Heart

MANY OF US in this region know a little of one another's language. Most of the Pueblo Indians speak Spanish with a delightful Indian intonation. We Anglos have come to use many Spanish terms as naturally as we do our own. A few Spanish-Americans of the older generation can understand and speak at least one of the neighboring Indian languages.

Such a one was Cousin Canuto, the *primo* of Mrs. Apodaca. Cousin Canuto's ability to speak Tewa as well as Spanish and English obtained for him the high position of checker in one of Santa Fe's Serve Self markets. Even when he was receiving the unheard-of salary of two hundred dollars a month, he resigned to have more time for the higher things of life. He started a *tiendacita*—little store—in one room of his adobe home, thereby acquiring time to sing around the old wood-burning stove on winter nights and to water his forest of hollyhocks on summer afternoons.

A hopeless romantic, Cousin Canuto became involved with many startling affairs. He chanced to see two flying saucers in the blue New Mexican sky and he read about them in his favorite Spanish-language newspaper. From then on, Cousin Canuto was a man on fire with a dream. There was little doubt in his mind but that the saucers originated on some distant star and were manned by one or more diminutive citizens of that star. This naturally led to the even more thrilling supposition that the *plato*—saucer—would probably land among Cousin Canuto's blooming hollyhocks. And then came the terrible thought as to how he might be welcomed. "Of course," worried Cousin Canuto, "I would say, *'Bienvenido, Señor, mi casa es suya* —Welcome, sir, my house is yours!' But then there is just a possibility that he may not understand Spanish, nor Tewa, nor even English."

Cousin Canuto brooded over this barrier to courtesy for many days. At last a scintillating idea lightened his gloom. He remembered hearing of the sign language used in the early days.

Surely he could find an old Indian who would teach him the sign language that he might welcome the little man on the *plato*.

Early in August a few years ago, he borrowed the gangling steed of his *primo,* Pantalones Padilla, and started out. Equipped with saddlebags stuffed with María Lupita's good cooking, a roll of blankets, and his *guitarra,* he might have been Don Quixote himself, cantering through my yard.

Weeks passed and Cousin Canuto did not return. Occasionally letters were received, saying he was in Jémez, in Cochití, on lofty Ácoma and even in Albuquerque. Not a word did he say about the sign language.

By the third week in August, all Tenorio Flat was up in arms against Cousin Canuto. That is the time of year when responsible *papás* find a little extra work, if possible, to buy new shoes, blue overalls, bright dresses, and warm sweaters for the *muchachos* to wear when school opens. If *los papás* cannot find extra work, the *mamacitas* swathe their heads in flour sacks and help Anglo ladies to get their houses ready for winter.

But poor María Lupita could not do this, what with the seven *muchachos,* the *tiendacita,* and Cousin Canuto's forest of hollyhocks which needed endless buckets of water drawn from the blue-covered well.

Tenorio Flat held day and night conferences on the problem. At last it was decided that Mrs. Apodaca should take María Lupita and the two youngest children into her home and the others should be crammed somehow into other overflowing *casitas* of the neighborhood. All Tenorio Flat felt Cousin Canuto should have a much-needed lesson. It would serve him right to return to an empty house, a boarded-up *tiendacita,* and a family scattered to the four winds.

A few days before school opened, the wanderer cantered gayly into his deserted, hollyhock-drooping *placita.* In no time at all the hollyhocks revived, the boards over the windows came down, and his family scuttled home like nesting birds. What is more, his *muchachos* had the shiniest shoes, the bluest overalls, the brightest dresses, and the heaviest sweaters ever seen in the neighborhood. Furthermore, every child had a magnificent pencil box filled with assorted equipment for a prolonged scholastic career. Tenorio Flat wagged its head and rolled its eyes heavenward, baffled by the inexplicable.

A little later, Cousin Canuto, like a wandering Ulysses, came to the Little Adobe House to give an account of his wanderings.

"Did you learn the sign language?" I asked.

"*Sí*," nodded Cousin Canuto, "there were some old Indians who remembered a little of it. But at its best, I could see that it was a clumsy affair and not worth a man's time. As you know, Señora, the Indians of the Rio Grande speak three different languages and I know only the Tewa. Some of the younger Indians speak no Spanish and some of the older no English. Until I found the language of the heart, I was often at a loss as to how to converse with them.

"Would you believe it, Señora, hardly once in all those weeks did I have to sleep out in the open. Nearly always some Indian came along and gave me a bed in his *casita*. I gave away most of María Lupita's good cooking, so many times did the Indians ask me to eat with them. Sometimes we did not speak the same language, but we understood each other very well—far better, I might say, than when thoughts get smothered in many words. You see, Señora, the *guitarra* did the talking. That is a language any man can understand.

"I have made a great discovery, Señora. There is a language of the heart that is common to all. It speaks with the eyes and shines in the face and ripples like a brook with kind thoughts. Not even the little man on the *plato* could mistake that."

But I was not to be sidetracked. I felt I must uphold Tenorio Flat and its lesson for this hopeless romantic. "Poor María Lupita had a pretty hard time while you were away discovering the language of the heart," I complained. "Someone must have earned the money to send your children to school decently dressed."

Cousin Canuto's long fingers felt under the sweatband of his big hat. To my amazement, he pulled out folded bills and stacked them in neat piles. "For the taxes, for the wholesale grocers, for a shawl with fringe for María Lupita, for a party to celebrate my return, Señora. All the rest went for the *muchachos'* new school clothes and the fine pencil boxes.

"It was on the sand trail to Ácoma that I met the Anglo men who paint the pictures. I was riding my horse up the deep sand trail and singing to my *guitarra* as I rode. Those Anglo *pintores*—artists—almost took me prisoner. In their fine studio down in the valley, I posed for them many days. I was ashamed to take the money they gave me, but they said it was nothing. While they painted, I told them about the *guitarra* that everyone could understand. The best picture of all they called *The Language of the Heart.*

Tienda
Testing Ground

FOR SOME
years now, I have been watching the *tienda* that
Benito started, out in the dirt-road district. Step
by step, in its growth and in its vicissitudes, Benito's store has answered some of the questions
concerned Anglos are asking about our Spanish-
American neighbors.

The question voiced most frequently is:
"Will the young moderns among our Spanish-
American population be absorbed and their dis-
tinctive racial characteristics lost by acquiring
Anglo ways? Will money-making and competi-
tion spoil them?"

Benito is young and modern. The *tienda*
he started when he returned from war service
was not a *tiendacita*—little store. It was not in
one room of his house. It was in a building by

itself. There were shelves, bins, and a counter that held a cheap cash register. The stock consisted mostly of what the large Spanish-American population of the neighborhood might buy, and a small refrigerated meat counter.

In a little while, Anglos of the neighborhood were taking advantage of a *tienda* close at hand. Gradually, Benito stocked the commodities we needed—fresh fruits and vegetables and a deep freeze for frozen ones—cream, butter, and more expensive cuts of meat. He met the unpredictable emergencies of our households with electric bulbs and cords, a case of thread, and our favorite shampoo soap.

That *tienda* was a pleasant place to go. Many of us went almost every day, having acquired the day-by-day buying habits from our Spanish neighbors.

In Benito's homey, gay little store, we met our friends, black-shawled Señoras, *muchachos* after penny candy, and school children refreshing themselves with highly colored soda pop. We could stand around and chat as long as we liked. There was no sense of hurry. Benito was always smiling and interested in our various households. His store had taken on the quality of a native *tiendacita*. It was a community meeting place.

In a couple of years, parking places became hard to find downtown, especially after five o'clock. Then more and more Anglos who lived further up the *acequia* discovered that they could park in front of Benito's and do their shopping on the way home from work. Benito now had a "carriage trade." He met the situation by stocking the luxuries his new customers wanted. The checking-out counter space had to be doubled and a second cash register installed.

Benito went straightaway to Cousin Canuto and asked him to man the second cash register at a starting salary of a hundred dollars a month. Cousin Canuto deliberated the momentous question for some weeks and then gave his decision. . "A few years ago, I escaped a bigger monster of a cash register and bigger pay in the Serve Self market. Why should I go back into slavery for a little cash register and little pay? Besides, the Señoras need my *tiendacita*. It is too far for the ones in my *placita* to walk way down here."

Benito met this problem by teaching the intricacies of cash-register operation to Altagracia, his wife. As she had completed high school, she was fully prepared to master practically anything. He installed a little "rahdio" beside the cash register, that she might hear her favorite programs in between rush hours. Altagracia and her "rahdio" were great additions to the store. She was pretty to look at and she gave a feminine grace to the establishment.

And then something happened that any Anglo might have foreseen in the light of Benito's prosperity. A new supermarket was started not too far away. It was all chromium and plate glass, its endless shelves filled with the world's luxuries and necessities in bewildering profusion. A great space, all neatly cemented, offered convenient space for parking cars. "Poor Benito," everyone said, "he will lose all his customers."

First his "carriage trade" left him, then many of the neighborhood Anglos and even the black-shawled Señoras. We all sampled the elegance and prodigious variety of the new supermarket.

One by one, the Spanish-American customers returned to Benito. The super-*tienda* was a marvel, but it was no place to send a *muchacho* with a scribbled list in Spanish, to be filled by a clerk who didn't so much as know that *arroz* meant rice. Then we neighborhood Anglos returned, one by one, to the pleasant, homey little store. Finally, quite a few of the "carriage trade" came back, grinning self-consciously. "There's something more to buying groceries than picking out a basketful," one of them remarked. "The checkers in the market were polite and efficient. The Spanish language has a word for great stores like that—*demasiado*—too much."

One dark winter night of swirling snow, a long line of customers was waiting to be checked out by Altagracia. Benito had seven or eight of his most important "carriage trade" before his own counter. First in his line was a little Anglo girl, who presented a long scribbled list sent by her mother. Benito grinned at his waiting "carriage trade," picked up a basket and carefully filled the list. It made a heavy bagful for the child. Then he peered through the window at the dark night, the blinding snow, and cars hurrying homeward. "I'll just get the *muchacha* across the street," he said.

After what seemed a long time, he returned shaking snow from his white-coated shoulders. "Thought I'd better take her home," he explained. "The bag was too heavy and people were driving every which way."

Benito's "carriage trade" nodded understanding heads. There had been not a word of complaint.

That Carmencita
Wins Again

"WHAT DOES the tax paper say we paid on our *casita* last year?" Mr. Apodaca asked, holding this year's bill apprehensively in his hand.

"*Un momento,*" responded Mrs. Apodaca and dropped to her knees beside the bed. After some searching, she produced a small wooden box with the patina of years on its homemade sides. She rummaged about in its untidy collection of papers and produced, in triumph, last year's receipted payment of taxes. "Seven dollars and fifty cents in April and the same in November," she announced like an oracle. "Fifteen dollars for the year."

Mr. Apodaca tossed the new bill into the box as if he never wanted to see it again. "Nineteen dollars and twenty-seven cents this year! To what are we coming, Señora?"

That box of Mrs. Apodaca is a racial institution. It is referred to portentously as *"mi cajón—my box."* Every Señora of any upbringing in the old ways has her *cajón*. Señoras in Mexico, in California, in Texas, and in Arizona can produce almost any family document from *"mi cajón."* These all are hidden under beds and contain deeds to property, marriage and baptismal certificates, soldiers' honorable discharge papers, and yellowed clippings from Spanish language newspapers. *"Mi cajón"* is the family safe deposit box. It is more than that. It is the symbol of *mamacita's* position of responsibility in the family.

"They fill up," sighed Mrs. Apodaca, struggling to push a stout wooden peg through a staple that fastened down the lid. "It's that Carmencita! All her report cards from school, all the letters about prizes in the contests, and now the mention of honor for the picture she painted for the school art show. Every day she has to open *mi cajón* to see if that mention of honor is still safe."

In a few days Carmencita asked to go with me when I had papers to put in my "safety deposit box." Her big eyes nearly popped from her head when she saw the heavy doors, the rows of shining boxes and the attendant who used two keys to open the box. Here was safety, indeed! And I knew it would be only a matter of days before she, too, would sign her name grandly on an entrance card, produce a shining key and watch the impregnable open at her request. There would be another key to jangle with the one to her box in the U Esse Post Office.

And then something happened. No new key jingled on the chain about Carmencita's neck. She went about sad-eyed and drooping, and barely spoke as we passed.

Mrs. Apodaca drooped, too. Wrapped in her oldest shawl, she stalked through my yard, simply lost in the part she was playing of a *mamá* who was upholding family tradition—against great odds.

Unhappily, one day I was forced to listen to the points at issue. "That *cajón*," Carmencita was saying, "an old wooden box that doesn't even lock and that anyone could carry away under his arm!"

"Every Señora has her *cajón*," retorted her mother. "Never in all my life did I ever hear of one being robbed by a thief or carried away by a prowler. But banks—just listen to the *rahdio* and you can hear they are robbed almost every day."

Carmencita ignored that argument. "Remember the flood we had a few years ago, when the roof fell in and water was all over the floor. Do you think I want my mention of honor in a *cajón* floating around in the water? Or suppose we had a fire! What would become of your *cajón* then?"

"A *mamá* always saves her *cajón*—first," replied Mrs. Apodaca, tight of lip and straight of back. "Some day when you are a great *pintora* people will want to see this first mention of honor. It will be in *mi cajón*."

I glanced at the spot where the mention of honor picture hung in all its glory beside the geranium window, and it seemed to me that mother and daughter were crossing bridges that would never materialize.

Suddenly, in a few days, all was sunshine in Tenorio Flat. Mrs. Apodaca, her head bound with a flour sack, and whitewash brush in hand whisked through my yard. "I go to whitewash Mees Boggers," she announced happily. "I go to earn money to buy Carmencita a sweater for winter—*verde*.

A few minutes behind her trotted Carmencita, her long legs twinkling. "I go to wash windows for Mrs. Forest Ranger," she tossed back over a disappearing shoulder. "I earn money to buy *mamacita* a pair of new shoes—stylish."

Never was early autumn sun so warm nor breeze so caressing. Hollyhocks fluttered ballet skirts, and a house finch sang a farewell song in the pear tree.

Some days later, Mrs. Apodaca gave me the explanation of this delightful state of affairs. "The mention of honor is in *mi cajón*," she rejoiced. "That Carmencita is content with only a copy of it in her safety deposit. You see, Señora, she had something made she says is a stataphote."

The Fifth
Ear of Corn

SNOW
was falling around the Little Adobe House, as
five of us sat before the corner fireplace. Blazing piñón logs painted red shadows on plain
white walls. The fire and the chile-red candles
were the only light in the night-filled room.

Out of a comfortable silence, the poet said:
"Why are we five here in this strange land,
perched high on the apron of the Rockies? And
why do we stay on and on? Not one of us was
born here. Not one of us but has left established
roots—home, friends, professions, greater oppor-
tunities to make money. What charm does this
land hold over us? Why does it draw certain
people like a magnet and never let go of them?"

The artist mentioned scenery and color.
He spoke with singing words of dark, sky-touch-
ing mountains topped with snow, of valleys

reflecting a sea of ever-changing light, of the incredible blue that the atmosphere holds like dyestuff in a bowl.

But deep in our hearts, we knew this was not the answer. Someone spoke of the Alps, of the High Sierras of California, and the glorious tableland where Popo lifts its austere head over a lavish outpouring of raw pigment.

The rancher drawled that maybe it was the climate, the thin dry air, the orderly progress of the seasons, the snows that sank gently into the adobe soil because of the vast number of sun-filled days in the year. The sunshine, that was it—sun soaking into old adobe walls and into the heart of man.

But all of us had wandered in far places. We could think of many lands where the seasons progress gently from lilac bloom to snow crystals, where golden sunlight mellows the heart of man.

After a long silence in which the little, deep-set windows rattled in the wind, the anthropologist spoke: "Maybe it is the people rooted here, the people of Spanish heritage, simple, gracious and colorful in a culture so much older than our own. And the Pueblo Indians, living serene of face in a still older culture."

But that was not it, we decided reluctantly.

Some of us could remember Spanish villages in Mexico and the beauty of scarlet-skirted Tarascan Indian women in Mexico's misty Lake Country.

The poet broke in on our thoughts. "It is the mystery of the place," he said. "Over it broods the shadow of The People Who Are Gone. Who knows anything about this country? A few centers of population, a few adobe villages and Indian pueblos, a few highways and a maze of dirt roads! And beyond that—what? Who built the great, five-storied cities whose ruins we find scattered in desolate places? They had winding passageways, vast circular council chambers, and a skillful system of irrigating ditches. Scholars have spent their lives trying to piece together a few scraps of evidence. Where did these people go and why?"

But it was not the all-pervading mystery of the land for which we had left homes and professions. The Little Adobe House echoed with our laughter and the piñón fire chuckled with us.

The social worker's glance rested on the five ears of Indian corn that hang by every well-regulated New Mexican fireside. The five differently colored ears represent the Indian's five

—not four—directions, east, west, north, south, and up. Why they do not represent their sixth direction—down—is another mystery.

"Maybe what we are talking about is symbolized by that fifth ear of corn, the up direction," she said slowly. "The uncompassed, the intangible direction!"

On the shoulders of all of us pressed again the remembrance of the heavy weight of ambitions, the straining and frantic hurry we had known in other places. Here, in our shining mesa land we had found that a little mud house can shut out the wind and the cold as well as can the most luxurious of housing. We had discovered that red beans in a pot are as acceptable to a walk-whetted appetite as the most costly of banquets. We knew that a tiny fireplace, no bigger than a bee-hive, and a few sticks of piñón wood could enfold companionship as warm and gay as the blazing wood itself. It took so little effort to provide these simple things. Here we had time to reach for some of the intangibles.

"Do you know," the artist laughed, "that never in my life have I worked so hard as I have here? Only there is no pressure behind it. Even I can see it is my best work and it is only the beginning. Probably it's true of all of us."

"But that isn't the whole story," contended the poet. "Why does our work seem almost effortless? Why are we doing more and better work?"

"Well," drawled the rancher, "I don't know about you people, but there's something here that's exciting, something that says, 'Anything could happen here.'"

"Expectancy," cried the artist. "That's it! I never get up in the morning, but I feel it. I never so much as walk to the Plaza, but I feel it. That is the magnet that draws us and holds us. That is why we work without any sense of pressure. Expectancy is what that fifth ear of Indian corn, the up direction, represents."

Son of Koshare

A COUPLE of years ago disappeared Koshare, the chile-eating, candle-snuffing cat who gave a Spanish lilt to my Little Adobe House. One cold winter morning he sauntered elegantly up the path beside the frozen water ditch, never to be seen again.

Immediately people I knew and people I didn't know came in streams to remedy the catless situation. Some came in cars with baskets filled with entrancing kittens. I could choose one or two or keep the whole basketful. Others came on foot with a kitten's head protruding from a paper bag. Still others conjured kittens from overcoat pockets or from beneath a buttoned sweater—Siamese kittens, long-haired Persians, short-haired kittens with golden eyes.

Then the news spread to distant states.

There were special delivery letters, telegrams, and long-distance telephone calls. "Why not try a dog this time? How about a dachshund or a cocker?" One word and the puppy would be shipped by air.

To all I gave a million thanks, but it was, "No, no, no." The reason was that I had already settled with myself for no less than the *hijo*—son—of Koshare, and I was certain that he would appear in the due course of time. But the weeks and the months passed without an heir apparent claiming the Navaho saddle blanket before the corner fireplace.

Wherever I went in the neighborhood, I kept an eye beamed for tiger cats with tremendous whiskers, a Philip the Second ruff, and the elegance of a Spanish grandee.

I discovered one in Benito's neighborhood store. Benito said I was welcome to the cat as it was given to knocking down boxes of soap powder and cans of tomatoes from the shelves. But the Señora of Benito did not object to groceries strewn over the floor. When I picked up the kitten, she wept and assailed the grinning Benito with a torrent of outraged Spanish which caused me to retreat in disorder.

Months later when I was almost tempted to wire for the dachshund or cocker, little Diolinda Alire appeared with her skirt gathered up in a bag. In the bag was a tiny kitten. It was the *hijo, verdad!* The same tremendous whiskers, the promise of a Philip the Second ruff, the same black-and-gray stripes underlaid with good adobe russet! "It's the *hijo de* Koshare," I shouted, taking the heir apparent in my arms.

Diolinda smiled politely. *"No es el hijo,"* she explained with great exactitude and dignity. "His mother is Koshare's daughter." So it was a *nieto*—grandson—of the old grandee and not a son. What difference did a generation make? Hijo de Koshare, the new kitten in the Little Adobe House has remained to this day.

But with the exception of whiskers, ruff, and adobe russet accents, Hijo is no more like his illustrious grandsire than the dachshund would have been. Through the months he has become half again as large as Koshare and his beautiful coat is a good, sober gray with sedate trimmings of black and russet. Under his chin he has acquired the semblance of a white collar with vestee attached. It gives him the aspect of a Puritan worthy. In a house filled with yellows and reds and bright blues, he looks as much out of place as a Pilgrim father stranded on a peak of Darien.

He eats no chile-flavored vegetables, but prefers a substantial meat stew thickened with Scotch oats. He blinks scandalized eyes when I light the blue candles one by one. Not an exhibitionist like his ancestor, he visibly tolerates guests with exemplary fortitude. But for all his restrained exterior, he is the most affectionate little animal I have ever known. When snow is on the ground, he follows me (disapproval registered in each uplifted cold paw) as I sweep paths and bring in piñón wood. I have to lock him in the house when I go downtown or he would follow me (disapproving but valiant) through traffic to the Plaza. When I return, I find him sitting in the deep-set little window, peering out anxiously through the gathering dusk. He greets me with an ecstatic "oo-oo-ooo" and purrs in a series of explosions.

For Hijo is a talking cat. As such, the telephone is his constant delight. As I am on a party line, one ring means Tenorio Flat and two rings mean my *casita*. But Hijo insists that I answer them all.

"OO-OO-OOO," he insists.

"One ring isn't ours," I grumble. "You're smart enough to learn that."

"OO-OO-OOO, it might be," he persists hopefully. Nights when I have settled down to sleep, I can hear him answering any and all telephone rings. He clumps noisily across the floor, scrambles into a chair by the 'phone and dutifully, in tones comically like my own, answers with prolonged oo-oo-oos. His voice grows louder and louder as the bell continues to ring.

Along about midnight, he plays a sedate game of bowling with a big, hard-rubber ball that he somehow manages to find no matter where I hide it. He has become an expert in the game as he manages to hit with a resounding crash, every chair and table leg in the room. Along about morning he jumps into the old rocker by the fireplace. That rocker has a squeak that is like the tearing of cloth. Hijo rocks back and forth like some comfort-loving grandmother. As he rocks, the chair squeaks and squeaks discordantly.

On summer nights, he sleeps in the open window by the pear tree. As my bed is directly under that window, I am regaled at intervals all night with custodial comments of what goes on in the darkened yard.

"OO-OO-OOO," exclaims Hijo, "a dog is passing by. I do not approve of dogs. OO-OO-OOO, people passing through our yard. Late movies!"

Once he awakened me with hissing accents. Something monstrous had appeared. His call was so amazed that I peered out, myself, and could not believe my eyes. Two lop-eared burros, one behind the other, were plodding, like ghosts of another day, past the Little Adobe House. No one keeps burros in the neighborhood now. They must have come in from some native village to take in the sights of urban Santa Fé.

Now I am awaiting some purple-shadowed night of murky witchery when Hijo, from his sentry box in the deep-set window, will give me his excited commentary, "OO-OO-OOO, a dinosaur, a dinosaur is slithering through our yard."

Violeta
Beauty Shop

BEFORE
Hijo took over the Little Adobe House, it had
the only telephone in this part of Tenorio Flat
and we had not progressed to the dial system.
My neighbors were considerate in asking to use
the telephone. No young people made or broke
dates. Occasionally Mrs. Apodaca or another
Señora came with a crumpled bit of paper con-
taining telephone numbers and made the fact
known that she was open for a day or two of
house-cleaning. There were many protestations
for "molesting" me.

If it had not been for the Violeta Beauty
Shop, my telephone at that time would have
offered few diversions. It was intriguing to call
a number and, after a prolonged delay, hear a
soft Spanish voice answer, "Violeta Beauty

Shop." Why, when I had given the number of the grocer or the gas company, the Violeta Beauty Shop should answer I will never know. Perhaps the operator felt a continual longing for a shampoo or a manicure and plugged in the number of her favorite shop.

It was also intriguing to receive gratuitous advice on any problem arising. Once when my roof sprang a leak following a downpour, I tried to call the roofing man. "I will ring heem," the same soft voice answered, "but already I ring heem a million times. *Ay de mí*, every roof in Santa Fé is leaking, even the roof *del Gobernador*."

But one summer night my telephone was busy, hour after hour. I had gone to bed late, anticipating a restful sleep under open windows where the pear tree rustles to night breezes and stars make an exact pattern over the roof line of a projecting ell. I was dozing off when I felt someone standing under the open window.

I have a friend who often experiences her most profound thoughts in the dead of night and rushes to tell me of them. I raised myself on an elbow and, addressing a shadowy form outside, said sleepily but firmly: "No, no, Susan, I am much too sleepy to discuss Ralph Waldo Emerson tonight—or life at Walden Pond, or even the poems of Emily Dickinson. Dear Susan, go home."

"Thees is not Susana," a voice from the shadows answered. "Is Mrs. Apodaca. Mrs. Vigil has new baby girl. Please let me use *el teléfono* and call godparents."

I rushed to open the door. Mrs. Apodaca called a number and poured out a rapturous description of what seemed to be an utterly new manifestation. "*Tan* sweet," repeated Mrs. Apodaca over and over again. "That *angelita* —*tan, tan* sweet."

Scarcely had I dozed off again before another timid voice asked permission to use *el teléfono*. I opened the door for another black-shawled figure. It seemed that grandparents in Mora must be informed. There was some difficulty attendant on this call as it was long distance. The price had to be determined from the operator, coins tightly tied in the corner of a shawl had to be extracted and the exact change deposited on my table before the call could be placed. As the grandparents in Mora had no telephone, the keeper of the local store had to be routed from his bed and pledged to immediate delivery of the glad tidings.

At this, I sent word to Tenorio Flat that my door would be left unlocked and a night light and *el teléfono* awaited their pleasure, but I wished to sleep. All night, dark figures flitted in and out. *Primos* were called as far away as Truchas and Trampas. *Amigos* were called in every part of town. Unknown people floated in and out. Unknown voices talked softly over the telephone. No one paid the slightest attention to the recumbent figure on the couch. It was a strange night.

Shortly after the war, another *teléfono* appeared in this part of Tenorio Flat. My line became a party line. The telephone operators often rang me instead of the new subscriber. A voice would say, "I want to talk to Ermelinda. Will you, *por favor*, go and get her?"

"But I don't know Ermelinda nor where she lives."

"She live up the hill around to the left where the deetch runs in peoples' back yards."

As I hesitated, the voice would have an after thought. "Is this María Tranquila?"

Evidently María Tranquila called far-flung Tenorio Flat to the phone. She also left the receiver off while she wandered calmly over hill and through arroyo, along ditches and past peoples' back yards to summon Ermelindas and other euphonious names to prolonged conversations about nothing at all.

María Tranquila had other enchanting ways with a telephone. Being the owner of a record player, she would take the receiver down, turn up the player and give half-hour concerts to friends on the outskirts of town.

Trying to place an occasional call, I have become proficient in a new aspect of linguistics —teen-age Spanish that is neither Spanish nor English.

" 'Allo, Escolástica. ¿Cómo está? You know what? *Tengo muchas* dates with that new fello."

"What you wear?"

"New dress—*azul*. He has truckie. We go to dance in Algodones. On La Bajada, *la luz*—the light—goes out and *la* engine stop. Along comes another truckie and poosha-le and poola-le us home. Now I theenk I not have dates with heem again. My *mamá* was *furiosa*. Not once this week I get to movies. Anyway, he is the old fello *de* Gracie. She is *furiosa también*—also."

Gusty breathing pulsates over the wires and then a sad silence. At last, "Now you tell me, Escolástica, what you be didding." It goes on and on.

Thirty-eight minutes later, I make a final attempt to catch the last grocery delivery of the day. Breathlessly I place a call. "Violeta Beauty Shop," a soft voice answers.

Off the Paved Roads

THE MOST
welcome words anyone can say to me as we jaunt
about our region, are: "Let's see where that
little dirt road goes."

Late in September, we sighed with relief
as we left the smooth standardized highway to
bump through the ruts of a road we had never
explored. It was fairly good at first, but, as we
approached the Rio Grande, we found ourselves
churning wildly through dry sandy washes or
pushing the little car up the steep banks of sal-
mon-colored arroyos. With the highway only a
few miles back of us, we had dropped back a
couple of centuries where Spanish-speaking
people still lived on primitive *ranchitos* or con-
gregated in lovely but poor adobe villages. Aside
from remembered beauty, this road promised
little material for winter musings.

The village we went through looked like a stage setting with the autumn sun shining in golden brush strokes along sagging adobe walls hung with scarlet chile strands. Front yards still showed yellow marigolds and clumps of pink and lavender asters. Our progress along the village street was a series of stops and starts, to avoid farm animals dozing on the soft, warm sand or wandering aimlessly about. Everywhere the villagers were leaning against sunny walls or sitting on *portales* or moving from house to house for that sociability which is a distinctive part of their natures. Only the vivid colors were active. All else was wrapped in an atmosphere of quietude and endless time.

But on the *ranchitos* was a mild activity. Water, portioned out from the river, filled a network of little ditches which ran languidly in all directions. Apples hung red on gnarled old trees. Poorly clad *muchachos* climbed and filled battered tin pails with the small-sized harvest. From tree to tree, their voices rose as gayly as piñón jays on the wing.

"It's beautiful," sighed my companion, "but it's all gradually running down like a music box that needs winding."

As we turned into a rutted side road that

led to an adobe ranch house at some distance, a shining little brown horse came cantering across the browning fields. On his back sat a small Spanish-American boy in new overalls and a bright-blue shirt. Behind the boy was evidently a baby brother, with his fat legs sticking straight out on either side and his fat arms stretched as far as they would reach around his brother's waist. Behind the horse trotted a colt with white splotches along its sides. Behind the horses, two dogs dashed back and forth viewing the landscape with limpid eyes.

The sun-drenched cavalcade came to a full stop. "Do you live here?" we asked, thinking the *ranchito* we had reached looked a little too prosperous to belong to his people.

"*Sí,*" grinned the young *caballero* with a flash of white teeth, "in the adobe under the big cottonwood trees, and in all the other houses you see live my uncles and my grandmother and my married sisters and brothers."

Here was a strange state of affairs. Whoever heard of a Spanish-American family having land enough for three generations and several families to live on? As we continued along the road toward the big cottonwood trees, we saw unobtrusive evidences of an activity that seemed alien to this two-hundred-year-old setting. Farming tools were not battered and worn. Ditches had cement intakes and outlets. Orchards had been pruned and fields contour-ploughed.

The house under the cottonwood trees was evidently of great age, but it did not sag and its walls were smooth with adobe plaster. Out of a blue-painted door came a smiling young woman who offered us drinks of cool well-water and a red willow basket heaped with white grapes and enormous red apples.

Little by little, as we sat under the copper-leaved cottonwoods, the story came out. The *ranchito* had always belonged to this family, but they could never make it produce enough for one group of them and the "old ones." Then, along, one day came an Anglo lady who loved the great sweep of unproductive land and bought it from them. She must have had a golden tongue, because Spanish-American families will seldom part with their watered lands.

As the Anglo lady needed help, she moved in, one by one, the married uncles and the grandparents. Together they made the place produce more and more. After they had all lived and worked side-by-side for many years, the Anglo lady left them. But in her will she returned the place to the family.

As we bumped homeward along the river road, we talked of the landmark one unknown woman had left beside the old river of romance. "I doubt if such a story could be found along a standardized highway," mused my companion. "That woman did not change the landscape nor the people. That family will always be *paisanos* —country people—with all their inherent traditions and love of the *tierra* still intact. I doubt if she thought of appointing a committee or a board of trustees. She left the regimented highway of philanthropic thought and took to the little dirt road of the individual. Perhaps that is what is wrong with the human race today. We've built standardized highways for almost every contact with our brothers—socially, educationally, philanthropically. Maybe we need to bump along the dirt road of the individual.

Across the valley, we watched the Jémez Mountains turn from mulberry blue to bright wistaria as the sun hurried westward toward the buttes and mesas of Navaho Land. We thought of that vast domain with only a few miles of paved highway. We thought of the years and the effort and the millions that had been poured out there in an attempt to make the tribesmen "regular Americans." Evidently "The People" —all 65,000 of them—were still adverse to becoming case numbers.

"Back in the realm of serial numbers," my companion snorted as we returned to the highway. "At least we have one comfort. We each live on roads that bear no street signs and in houses that show no numbers."

A Shepherding Land

THIS REGION of northern New Mexico, from earliest Spanish-colonial days to the present time, has been a land of shepherds. The whole country shares in this shepherding quality. Winds herd slow-moving white clouds across illimitable blue meadows overhead. Mountains inclose sun-singing valleys, mesa tops, and deep arroyos in a protecting fold. Even our thick-walled adobe houses repeat comfortably this shepherding theme.

I like to remember many years ago, when, as a visitor, I first saw what was to become my beloved land, I came in through flocks of sheep. It was early spring and, as we traveled along beguiling roads, we threaded our way through unhurried flocks. The sheep moved sedately, but the young lambs leaped with stiff-legged exuberance into the sparkling air. They were woolly exclamation points, punctuating the gentle scene.

To this day, in spite of natural beauties seen again and again with increasing joy, sheep, shepherded by dark, silent men moving across a color-filled landscape, remain the peak of visual enjoyment. My cry of "Sheep, sheep, sheep!" has become a paean of delight.

Numbers do not count. The family flock, guided by a manfully-striding Spanish village lad toward a grassy plot along a hesitant stream, is just as heart-warming as flocks of hundreds and thousands I have seen.

Once, in November, when Santa Fe had seen no snow, we made a last dash of the season for the Chama country, a hundred miles away on the Colorado line. But the day and night before we started, unheralded snow had fallen there. Great peaks along Cumbres Pass reared white and hard as alabaster against a blue, cloudless sky. All traffic through the pass had been halted.

Out of the canyons and down the foothills poured flocks of thousands of sheep. Shepherds were driving them incessantly, and rocks rolled under scrambling feet. The air quivered with b-a-a-ings. When, at last, a flock reached the brown stubble of flat, sun-filled meadows along the river, they lay and rested like inanimate rocks. Then would come the clatter of another flock tumbling down the hillsides, popping out of canyons and from behind cliffs.

After each shepherd had counted his sheep, at rest in the warm meadow, and wiped the sweat of effort and suspense from his face, he walked solemnly forward to greet with handshakings and excited exclamations the latest arrived *pastor*. The herders' eyes would linger on the sheep, safe in the sun-filled valley. Then they would turn and look upward toward the glittering barricade of snowy peak against peak and shake their heads and smile with triumph.

In another autumn, we were taking our first prowl through the tangled dirt roads of Navaho Land. Night found us miles from any settlement. Winds whined between barren cliffs. The sky was filled with low, sodden clouds promising rain. A few indecisive stars peeked forlornly around the edges of cloud banks. We were cold, hungry, and covered with the grime of dusty travel.

Then we saw a great fire of juniper beside a water ditch. Its flame was so red that it turned the branches of cottonwood trees to agate and the wool of clustered sheep to pink. Around the fire sat a dozen or so Navahos, keeping watch over the flock they evidently were moving to a lower level. Children huddled under their mothers' heavy shawls. The scent of supper cooking came teasingly to our nostrils. As we drove slowly past them down an unknown road, we heard the Navaho men singing one of their interminable songs. Somehow we felt comforted and refreshed by sight of huddled sheep around a ruddy fire, and by dark-faced singing shepherds with pellets of uncut turquoise swinging in their ears.

A few miles farther on, a Navaho on horseback appeared like an apparition and guided us to a place "where they are good to people." Good, indeed, they were! Water hissed in an enormous bathtub. Beds heaped with woolly blankets stood side by side in a big bare room.

Of all the men who labor in my beloved land, the shepherds have the deepest place in my heart. Ofter I have wished I could paint those patient, knowing shepherds with their eyes lifted to distant mountains. For that reason, I was overjoyed to receive a print of Peter Hurd's *El Pastor*. The shepherd is a short, squat man in clothing that has been drenched and baked by the elements, and slept in so long it seems another skin. He stands with his head thrown back looking at the unpredictable sky and begging it to caress the dry earth with moisture. In his left hand are his big battered hat and shepherd's crook. His right arm is stretched full length toward the sky and the hand so lifted is wide open.

The New Mexican shepherds kept the tiny flickering flame of European civilization ablaze in a land whose boundaries no one knew. Their flocks fed and clothed the first Spanish settlers hundreds of desert miles from a base of supplies. Woolly flocks soon overflowed to the neighboring Indians. Among the Navahos the results in weaving have become world famous. All this the uplifted open hand has given. No wonder this is a shepherding land.

Flicker's Feather

MY Spanish-American and Indian friends have taught me something about the giving of gifts. Oddly enough, they support Mr. Emerson's statements that a "Man's biography is conveyed in his gift," and that "there are persons from whom we always expect fairy tokens."

One cold winter night, when I was trudging home from the plaza through the heaviest snowfall of the year, Mrs. Apodaca rapped on her window and beckoned me to come in. Then she put a carefully wrapped hot platter in my mittened hands.

"Tonight, I make too many *enchiladas,* Señora; perhaps you like one for your supper." This was, of course, polite fiction, as there are never too many *enchiladas* in *casita* Apodaca.

With a red-winged fire in the corner fireplace, by the light of two candles, I sat with tray on knee and savored my neighbor's gift. The huge blue-corn *tortilla* was wrapped around bits of meat, mashed brown beans, and snippets of vegetables. Over it frothed a deluge of melted cheese into a scarlet sauce, *muy, muy picante* with pounded chile paste.

While the white locust tree tapped importunate fingers against the geranium window and snow unrolled like a scroll along flat roofs, I thought how much of Mrs. Apodaca's biography was contained in that gift. As a child, her brown fingers had learned the pat-pat of *tortilla*-making, had learned to string the waxy red peppers to dry against brown walls, had ground the blue corn.

I remembered standing on the high rock of Ácoma one Christmas day, when Indian women filled my arms with their beautiful pottery. That pottery was their biography, too. In it were centered the skills of generations of craftsmen. Its designs repeated the traditions and interpretations of a great people.

Alas! when I wished to make a gift, how often I telephoned the bookshop, ordered a book, asked to have it gift-wrapped and mailed.

About all of my biography that gift held was my signature on a check in payment.

There was a gift I once made, which, if it did not contain my biography, at least contained a goodly portion of that fairy-token quality Mr. Emerson recommends.

We had wandered into Navaho country in November. We were strictly on our own at that season, for there were no eating places, no hotels, few trading posts open. Against these conditions we had provided ourselves with warm blankets and a big box of food. Included in the cargo was a wholesale lot of stick candy in all flavors and colors, lollipops and peanut candy for any children we might meet.

Noon found us, in the course of time, on the brim of Canyon de Chelly. No one was there. The forest ranger had left for the winter. The Thunderbird Ranch had closed. We brought out our trusty box of food and munched crackers and cheese and big red apples as we leaned against pink rocks that skirted the raveling of dirt road along the rim.

Canyon de Chelly is a kind of Navaho Grand Canyon—but more accommodating to the capacity of the human mind. Down in the depths, a stream ran through treacherous quicksands. There were a few withered fields and leafless orchard trees. Smoke rose from a hogan. It was warm and still where we sat, the air so thin and permeated with color that it seemed we must be looking out from inside a gigantic, rainbow-hued soap bubble.

As we took the last cooky from the big, blue tin box, we heard, afar off, the grinding of wagon wheels coming slowly along the dirt road. Hoofs hit smartly against the rocks. Soon we could hear the singsong of Navaho conversation. A child laughed.

On an impulse, I snatched the empty blue cooky box and filled it full of stick candy—peppermint, cinnamon, and lemon. I jammed the lid on tight and put the box in the middle of the road. On top of the box I put an orange-red flicker's feather, one of two I had been wearing in my tam all the way into this enchanted land.

My companion and I dashed down a trail, hidden from the road, to continue our explorations on foot. At last we heard the wagon stop high above us on the rim road. Talk in Navaho rose and fell. Then wheels continued their way, grinding against stones and rocks.

It was late in the afternoon when we finally drove up to a trading post. All was dark inside with lanterns making orange-colored islands among the shadows. On benches along the walls Navahos sat talking, their big black hats blending with the darkness. It was better than any stage. All of Navaho living had its symbols here in the half-light—the hard-goods pole that fills up every winter with silver and turquoise jewelry pawned for sacks of flour and cans of lard; boxes of dye to keep Navaho shirts the bright hues they must be; babies on cradle-boards, children looking wistfully at stale candy; men huddled together, talking of sheep and blizzards and the latest master-thought from "Washingdon"; a woman swishing her sixteen-yard-wide skirt toward a bolt of crimson velveteen.

And then I spotted the flicker's feather in the big black hat of a little Navaho boy. He saw the feather in my tam at the same instant. His hand went up to his feather and mine to its mate. It was a salute that passed all barriers of age and race and language. It was a fairy token.

Part of
the Gift

FAR AHEAD, on the dusty road on the outskirts of Santa Fe, I could make out the outlines of an Indian woman padding along through the yellow-blossoming chamisa bushes. Everything looked unreal in the late summer atmosphere—even the swirls of purple asters that bordered the road.

Idly, I wondered what an Indian woman was doing so far from her pueblo, walking without hurry along my favorite hilltop road. For all the heavy burden she was carrying slung in a shawl between her shoulders, she walked as if she had a pleasant destination in view. She was part of the shimmering atmosphere, of the immense solitude and the quiet that lay like balm along the senses. Maybe she was not real, I decided, any more than the distant Ortiz Hills. In the unearthly glow of approaching autumn, they looked for all the world like a string of purple camels plodding single file through the desert.

At the top of the hill, where elfin piñón forests grow, I took a long circling trail that would provide the miles of walking such a day demanded. The Indian woman disappeared on a smaller circle.

I forgot all about her as I dipped down into pink arroyos, where quail scuttled to the shelter of trailside bushes and left intricate foot patterns in the rosy dust. Up on the mesa top in a thicket of juniper trees, two wild turkeys sat on a cinnamon-barked limb and contemplated the sunny valley below.

In a couple of hours, the trail bent back to the outskirts of Santa Fe and there was Emily's low adobe clinging to the hillside. Emily has lived alone in that adobe for many years. She says, with great glee, that she is the only person in the vicinity who neither paints nor writes. But all of us wish we knew our region as she does.

Her sprawling house has an inner patio, where pigeons spread white wings against the sky and where a little water ditch whispers between yellow marigolds and scarlet zinnias. On top of her flat roof, she has a lookout tower with a *kiva* ladder leading to it. Here she spends much of her time with sky and sun by day and with her star telescope by night.

Emily knows a great deal in an unacademic way about Indians. To her they are not anthropological specimens nor quaint survivals of a great people. Neither are they a minority group whose battles she feels called upon to fight. To her they are just people.

She has an intriguing habit of disappearing in her ancient car for months at a time. We do not worry about her because we know she is visiting around among the Indians much as she would visit her great-aunt Caroline, back in New England. Even the Navahos find her a hogan on their vast gaudy domain. She returns and tells with much complacency what a fine hogan she inhabited for a couple of months. It had a door, instead of a blanket over the entrance. And a wood floor and a small rusty cook stove! And Emily is no young adventurer in trousers and cowboy boots. She wears her graying locks in good Navaho style, tied up with colored yarn in a little bun behind.

As I turned into the patio, there sat Emily in the shade of a flowering tamarisk tree. There also sat the Indian woman who had not vanished into thin air as I had thought. Immediately I recognized her as Rafaelita, from a neighboring pueblo, one of the best pottery makers in the country. On the patio table were two of her finest bowls. They were as big as mixing bowls, but of graceful shape and covered with symbolic designs after the ancient manner. Such bowls are seldom seen these days outside of museums. Was Rafaelita trying to sell them to Emily? What could have happened to drive her to part with such priceless evidence of her skill?

After much talk and cooling refreshments, Rafaelita gathered her shawl about her and, with much handshaking set out to walk the long miles home. "Do let me drive you," Emily urged. Rafaelita refused gently, but positively.

Emily picked up the two great bowls and ran her hands appreciatively over their lovely contours, tracing a design with knowing fingers. "However can I thank you for these wonderful bowls?" she asked the Indian woman. "And remembering my birthday? I've never had such a beautiful gift." Then she added: "Why didn't you let me know, Rafaelita? I would have driven out to the pueblo and brought both you and the bowls in. It's many miles you have walked with those heavy bowls to carry. Now you must let me take you home."

Rafaelita smiled the inward-springing smile of the wise Indian who has lived many years. Looking into Emily's eyes on leaving, she said, as if surprised at our lack of understanding: "The walk is part of the gift."

In Such a Time
of Quietude

THERE COMES a time in northern New Mexico, that is neither autumn nor winter. Neither is it the heady resurgence of warmth and sunlight that is known in other regions as Indian summer. Rather, it is a pause and a cessation—a time when nature puts finger on lip and ponders visibly her own profound thoughts.

The Indians have caught something of this seasonal caesura. In their rhythmic and tireless dancing comes a curious break in tempo, difficult for the white man to comprehend or to imitate. Uplifted bronze arms and legs, wreathed with evergreen twigs, break the monotonous measure of full-throated *tombé* and rattling gourd with a pause so startling, it seems to leave the world suspended. Chanters bobbing about the uplifted Rain Pole, cease their monosyllabic song. No note breaks the silence.

It was in such a time of quietude that we found ourselves wandering slowly in some of the least known and remote areas of the State. Profligate aspen forests in mountain crevices long ago had tossed their minted gold to the winds. But, in the valleys, provident cottonwoods clung to their baser copper with miser's fingers. They lighted a far-flung coppery world that stretched, polished as a metal bowl, between turquoise sky and mountains.

Zía Pueblo on its mesa-top was a dream village—brown adobe house lolling against house in oblique sunlight. Sleepily it peered out from what, at a distance, seemed to be dull-red corduroy curtains hung along the mesa's edge. Closer approach proved the curtains to be strands of chiles, hung on wooden frames to dry—their autumnal crimson now dried to russet red.

Corn lay in varicolored heaps on flat rooftops. Spirals of pumpkin and squash hung suspended in the still air. In wattled corrals, horses stood, heads down. Children and pet sheep huddled in sunny corners. A woman stroked an intricate bird design on a red clay pot. All of time seemed given her for her labors. A whole village had caught nature's tempo.

Beyond Zía, where the great bowl of landscape was dented with jade and saffron arroyos, a flock of slowly moving sheep spread fan-like to block the road as far as the eye could see. Such was the effect of timelessness that we made no futile effort to part their numbers but adapted our small car's pace to theirs, stopping and starting as they moved gently ahead.

No authoritative dogs directed their movements. Four silent Navahos tossed an occasional pebble to right or left. Blue, purple, and yellow shirts bloomed like tropical flowers. Sheep moved along an old, old road shepherded by men with Asia in their eyes.

North and westward, the sense of suspended animation spread over a mile-high plateau. It was as if a race of giants, toiling through the centuries, had suddenly thrown down their tools and departed. The gargantuan statuary they had left stood all about. Battlemented cities spread over yellow cliffs. Obelisks pointed giant forefingers at the sky. A ship, carved from rust-red sandstone, seemed to move gently toward us over a sagebrush sea.

From behind serrated pinnacles came at long intervals a Navaho on horseback, the beat of hoofs muffled in deep sand. Or a Navaho woman, her full skirts blowing, passed over a hilltop, her stride free and powerful as the country she traversed. At nightfall, over roads as interwoven as a spider's web, white covered wagons converged like so many moths and flickered off across the dark, junipered hills.

Could it be, we asked ourselves, that we had by chance stumbled on a Navaho Yeibichai? Our little car joined the procession of slowly moving wagons. Out of the darkness, other Navahos—men, women, and children on horseback —appeared. Starlight caught the glint of silver belts and danced on swaying necklaces of turquoise-studded silver. Up the dry bed of a stream we crawled, knowing that even a moment's hesitation would sink us axle deep in sand.

In a dark wooded valley, a fire burned red before a shadowy hogan. Almost like magic, the covered wagons took their places with others already there, in a great semicircle that nearly filled the little valley. In the center the great fire blazed higher and higher. In front of each wagon, other small fires leaped into flame like stars around that central light that painted the hillsides red.

We were the only Anglos there. Gratefully we obliterated ourselves in the deep shadow cast by the hogan. Here, through a haze of juniper smoke, lighted by leaping, resinous flame, we saw, until almost morning, the drama of ancient America.

But the drama was not in the chanting as much as it was in the people, both chanters and spectators. It was in the faces of the women as they sat with their big-eyed children under the arch of hooded wagons. It was in big-hatted, blanket-wrapped men wandering from fire to fire. It was in their greetings and conversations pitched in singsong Navaho. It was in their laughter. It turned the mind back to Asia and those nomads who, with their flocks, followed the green grass when the world was young. It was the drama of a great people, holding tenaciously in one hand the symbolism of an ancient race, and with the other hand reaching out for modern tractors and deep flowing wells.

> In beauty I walk,
> with beauty before me,
> below me,
> above me,
> behind me,
> all around me.

The time of tranquillity at last had fitting words in the Navaho tongue.

Cobwebs
and Cables

A FEW NIGHTS before Christmas, Cousin Canuto came to pay me a holiday visit. A pink geranium was fastened to his sheepskin jacket, a plume of pine needles waved on his big hat and his eyes twinkled like candle flame in my shadowy room.

As he settled himself in the big rocker, he glanced with evident delight at the blue spruce, silver fir, and piñón branches that decorated the place from ceiling beams to floor line. It was a bower of greenery and fragrance. Cousin Canuto chuckled. "Do you remember, Señora, the year you decided to break all the customs of Christmas around the Little Adobe House? We Spanish have a proverb that says: 'Customs are first cobwebs and then cables.' Sometimes it is good to break even happy customs that they do not turn into cables."

We sat in companionable silence while the

piñón logs whispered their purring song of golden hills and limitless sky.

"It is a good night for story telling," said Cousin Canuto. "Would you like to hear the story of a custom that grew into terrible cables and how those cables were broken in a wonderful way to bring happiness to everyone?"

At my eager nod, Cousin Canuto drew a handful of piñón nuts from his pocket and started. "It happened when I was a young man and still lived in the little village far back in the mountains, where the 'Old One' still has his home. In that village lived two girls *muy, muy lindas* and their names were Lucita and Paz. They sat side by side in the one-room adobe schoolhouse; they marched side by side in all the village processions. Together they learned all the old songs and old dances. They were *amigas* from the time they could walk. Also in the village lived two boys, Ignacio and Maclovio. They likewise had been *compadres* from *niño* days.

"*Naturalmente,* Señora, when these young people grew up, Ignacio married Lucita and Maclovio married Paz. It was a double wedding with the brides standing under a silken canopy. Ignacio helped Maclovio build a little adobe house for Paz and Maclovio helped Ignacio build one for Lucita. Soon there was a path worn in the dusty *tierra* between the two houses, so great was the passing back and forth between the young people.

"The young husbands soon wanted a better living for their families than their *ranchitos* could provide. In the autumn, Ignacio went to Colorado to work in the harvest and Maclovio went to the coal mines in the Cerrillos hills. They would return before Christmas with *dinero* in their pockets and many nice things for their families. Always Ignacio had a fine gift for Lucita, and Maclovio one he hoped was even finer for Paz. In no time at all, it became a *rivalidad* of giving with the young men buying finer and finer things and the young women beside themselves in the hope of having the present that would call forth the most exclamations from the village people.

"At last, Señora, came a climax. Ignacio, on his way home one year, stopped to see an Indian. That Indian had made a goatskin rug. It was the biggest rug anyone had ever seen and the hair was long and curly. To line the rug, the Indian had used a piece of old Navaho blanket that had been on the seat of his grandfather's wood wagon for years and years. The wife of the Indian had washed the blanket in *amole* root and the colors had come out soft and pretty. Two inches of red, with a kind of purple bloom on it, extended around the edge. But what made it a rug *magnifica* were two big, yellow glass eyes the Indian had fastened to the head. That rug cost Ignacio much *dinero.*

"The village people came one by one and in processions to see that goatskin rug with the big, yellow glass eyes. Lucita spread it on the floor in front of her corner fireplace. *Sí* and people from all the villages roundabout came to admire and exclaim. But Maclovio grinned and waited. Then he gave Paz the gift he had bought on his way home. He had found it in a secondhand lumber place.

"It was a big door with a looking glass on one side, such as you Anglos use for the room of the bath. When Paz saw it, she jumped up and down with joy, because she had never liked the front door to their *casita.* That door was an old, hand-carved thing that someone in the family had whittled out a hundred years ago. She had Maclovio carry it out to the goat shed and hang the new door in its place. Señora, people came from miles around to see that door with the looking glass on the outside turned toward the village street.

"Alas! People exclaimed more over that door than they did over the rug with the big, yellow glass eyes in the *casita* of Lucita. The path between the two houses filled with weeds and dead leaves. There was no more visiting back and forth. The women did not even speak when they met each other, and neither did the young men.

"Then followed a bad year for the two families. There was no sugar-beet crop in Colorado for Ignacio to harvest and the coal mines in the Cerrillos hills closed down. It looked as if they would have to eat chile and beans for Christmas and the *muchachos* would have no new shoes, let alone a few toys and sweets.

"Then without warning an Anglo lady appeared in the village. She was of the kind that is always prowling around hunting for old things —like our Mees Boggers. Some one sent her to see the goatskin rug of Lucita. The Anglo lady shuddered when she saw that fine big rug with big yellow glass eyes. But, when she saw the red lining showing along the edge, she turned it over fast and felt the weave and peered at the colors. 'It's an old Bayeta!' she screamed. She gave Lucita five twenty-dollar bills for just the lining of that goatskin rug.

"Then someone sent her to the house of Paz to see the fine front door with the looking glass turned to the village street. When she saw that, the Anglo lady cried in her pocket-handerchief and shook as if something terrible had happened to her. But she cried right out in the open when she saw the old hand-carved door in the goat shed. She gave Paz five twenty-dollar bills for it.

"Paz with the bills in her hand started across the snow-filled path to the house of Lucita. But Lucita had come half way across to meet Paz. They laughed and cried together.

"What a Christmas was that, Señora! Ignacio and Maclovio drove the long snowy miles to Santa Fe—together. They returned with sacks of flour and sugar and shoes and warm coats and candy and nuts for the *muchachos*. *Sí,* and candy and nuts for all the village children. *Sí,* and good warm shawls for Lucita and Paz—exactly alike."

Cousin Canuto hurried toward the door. "Too long I molest you, Señora." I stood in the piñón-bordered doorway to hear him singing on his way home under the Christmas stars. He was singing of *paz* and *amor*—peace and love.

The Bed of
Sabelita

SABELITA
living in a West Coast city, far from her New
Mexican mountain village, was left clinging to
a central idea under the impact of Anglo ways.
But it almost wrecked the Department of
Charities.

Miss Muggler's face took on the color and
consistency of slightly melted raspberry sher-
bet. Her tired blue eyes and the corrugations
of her grey hair were startlingly drab by contrast.
There was a new superintendent in the Department of Charities. He was young and revolu-
tionary. He talked of methods of which Miss
Muggler and her fellow district directors had
never heard, since they received their political
appointments back in the good old days.

Miss Muggler's carefully fitted youthful
dress threatened to burst its seams as she pon-
dered the reported outcry of the new superin-

tendent, "Heaven help me! I'll get rid of those hard-boiled antiques, priority or no priority!"

Only three years to go until she could retire decently on a pension after all her years of work. What if that young whippersnapper—?

In regimented rows at little tables sat Miss Muggler's women workers. A little rail separated the workers from the worked-upon. It might well have been a bottomless chasm. The worked-upon sat crowded together on backless benches and waited. Miss Muggler often remarked that time could hardly be an important factor in a charity recipient's life.

From time to time she lifted her tired eyes from the case record she was reading and surveyed with mounting distaste the growing jam of humanity on the backless benches. Miss Muggler called all her women workers by their last names. She said it was more businesslike.

"Montague," she screamed, "there's that old man Twitchell of yours. He's carrying the teeth we bought for him in his hand again. Call up the dentist and tell him we didn't spend twenty dollars of the taxpayers' money for teeth to be carried around in the hand."

"Pointdexter, run that begger, Sabelita, out. Tell her no more *leche* and no more *provi-*

siones until she tells us where that worthless, deserting husband of hers is. I bet he's living right there in the house."

As she issued stentorian orders, Miss Muggler shelled peanuts, popping them into her mouth between war cries. Montague and Pointdexter dashed, with the nimbleness of youth, to the railing and talked in firm accents to Mr. Twitchell and Sabelita. The remaining two hundred and fifty crowded on the backless benches listened and watched in a kind of fascinated lethargy.

Swelling visibly, Miss Muggler studied her notes of the last staff meeting held by the new superintendent. For three mortal hours he had crammed "the case work approach" and other new-fangled follies down their reluctant throats.

"Young whippersnapper!" she exploded again. And then a crafty look came into her tired old eyes. "I'll have to string him along," she decided. "The inexperienced young upstart! I'll do him a case that is as full of rehabilitation as these beggars are full of lies."

There was her newest recruit, little Pointdexter, fresh from training school. She knew all the newfangled lingo and the kid could write. Up to now all of her impractical notions had been stepped on. But in a crisis, they might be useful.

"Pointdexter," she roared, "bring me the case record on that Sabelita woman of yours." She scanned it carefully, munching peanuts and humming mournfully a stanza of "Beulah Land" as was her custom when deeply interested.

"Pointdexter," she commented, "we've had that Sabelita of yours on our books for five or six years. Her *esposo* comes back every so often, and then he's off again. If we didn't support 'em, we wouldn't have so many desertions, I always say."

And then in tones she hoped were beguiling, "Pointdexter, how'd you like to tear loose on that case? Try everything you learned in training school. Write it up in your best style for the superintendent to see. Sort of a model case."

Little Pointdexter had reached that hectic place in her professional life when she was beginning to wonder if all the books she had read and all the erudite lectures she had attended were in vain. They didn't seem to fit into life as she found it in the Spanish-American district of her big city. Her big hazel eyes were daily growing more baffled and perplexed.

"Forget the rest of your file," urged Miss Muggler, "and go to town on Sabelita. If you do the kind of job I expect you to do, it'll mean a promotion for you."

After a week of frantic running here and there, Pointdexter dragged herself and her big brief case to her director's roll-top desk. "Well," demanded Miss Muggler, "well, what did you find out? Didn't let her drag in any of the neighbors' children as her own, did you? They'll do that."

Pointdexter shook her serious, braid-circled head. "I obtained all the birth certificates from the Bureau of Vital Statistics."

"And the *esposo!* I bet any amount of money he's living right there and working days!"

"No," Pointdexter disagreed mildly. "I've been in and out of the house at all hours—even at night. And I can tell by the way Sabelita acts. She's all broken up."

"But what does she say? You know Spanish. What does she talk about?"

"About her *esposo*. She loves him."

"Fiddlesticks," roared Miss Muggler.

"And she goes on and on about her *tierra* —her land. Until she came here a few years ago, she lived in a little mountain village in northern

New Mexico where every family had its apple trees and corn and chile patch and where goat bells tinkled all night long. And where there were dances and guitars strumming. She calls it her sweet-singing land. The poor thing is homesick."

"We'll send her back," Miss Muggler broke in, purple with the sudden easy solution. "Tell her to pack up tomorrow."

"She won't go. Her *esposo* might come back. She's making a *novena*. And she keeps a candle burning in a red glass before a statue of the Virgin of Guadalupe.

"Where she lives now, can't be much like her New Mexican mountain village," Pointdexter continued. "One of those sour, tumbledown courts in the industrial district. And the smell from the meat packer's place! Seven or eight people living in two rooms all around her."

"What kind of furniture does she have?"

"An old rusty gas range and a blue crib for the baby and a table with an oilcloth top and two old chairs and a couple of trunks and a pretty good radio that she's made two payments on, and a brass bed."

"A brass bed?"

"It's the apple of her eye. It's the biggest,

fanciest bed you ever saw. She and the five older children sleep in it. She's crocheted a cerise bedspread for it with the name of her New Mexican village right in the center. Everyone for blocks around comes to gape at that bed. She polishes the brass every day. It shines like the sun."

Miss Muggler was plainly bored. "Well, well, what's your plan?"

"If I could only get them moved into a nice little house on the edge of town where she could have a garden and a fruit tree or two. And the children could go to a nice little school and where maybe she could find some hour work and earn a little money."

"Okay," mumbled the director. "But not one new stick of furniture and not one cent of cash! It's the time of year our appropriation always runs low."

For weeks Miss Muggler scarcely saw her faithful worker, Pointdexter. All she knew was that the entire edge of the city was being scoured for the proper home for Sabelita.

Wet to the skin one day, Pointdexter dropped by the roll-top desk "I've found it," she gasped. "A house for Sabelita. Hundreds of miles I've traveled by bus and streetcar. But I found it—three rooms and bath and six fruit trees and a chicken pen and a place for a garden and a nice little school nearby and the teachers all so interested!"

"Dictate it all in the case record," demanded Miss Muggler, so carried away she signed a rent order for the new house that was three times the rental of the old. "Describe the kind of place you took the family out of and the nice new one and the fruit trees and how tickled Sabelita is."

"But she isn't," puzzled Pointdexter. "I don't think she wants to move. She cried and cried. She didn't exactly say she wouldn't—"

"She'd better not," roared Miss Muggler. If she acts stubborn, just tell her we'll cut off every cent of support we've been giving her. That'll fix her."

Pointdexter let herself out on that case record. Sitting on one foot, she dictated six rolls of highly descriptive matter. When it was all transcribed by her own secretary, Miss Muggler carried it herself to the superintendent's office.

Within an hour he was leaning flushed and pleased against her desk. "I'm calling a directors' staff meeting for Monday morning. It's the only decent piece of case work and the best piece of recording in the whole department."

Smiling and puffing, Miss Muggler took the afternoon off to wander in and out of her fellow directors' offices, there to gloat and hand about her precious case record. The young whippersnapper! She had been too smart for him.

Pointdexter was dashing madly about. She had gas, light, and water turned on in the new house. Saturday she reported that the brass bed and the other odds and ends had left by transfer truck for the new location. She, herself, was taking the family out by bus to get them settled.

On Monday, when Miss Muggler returned from a highly satisfactory staff meeting, which included the line-by-line reading of the model case and the enthusiastic compliments of the superintendent, she noted a new face at the extreme end of one of the backless benches. "See what that dickey bird wants," she roared at her secretary. Flushed with victory, she got out her powder puff and toned down the exuberance of her complexion.

"It's the landlord of the house Miss Pointdexter rented out on the edge of town. He says the family moved out in the night, Saturday, and we've got to pay him another month's rent as he lost a good tenant on the deal with us."

Like a stricken thing, Pointdexter grabbed her big brief case and started on the run. The director's voice followed her down the hall. "If you can find that Sabelita, you bring her right to my desk."

She was soon back, dragging the shawled and clearly unrepentant Sabelita by the hand. Stolidly Sabelita spread out her long, full-gathered black skirts and rolled round, defiant eyes at the flushed and panting *Inspectora*. "Why, why did you leave that nice little house and the fruit trees and the garden and move back to that awful hovel?"

Sabelita twisted a turquoise and silver ring on her brown finger. *"Mi esposo,"* she said in a stubborn voice, "could he find me in the place *rústico!* No?"

"What I want to know," exploded Miss Muggler, "is how she moved herself and all those children and all her household traps back to that hovel without a cent of cash."

Pointdexter questioned Sabelita, who burst into tearful Spanish.

"She says," translated little Pointdexter, "she sold her brass bed."

The Eyes See; the Heart Knows

THE CROOKED winding streets of Santa Fe have a daylight beauty. I, who never tire of sun-radiant adobe walls, would be the last to speak lightly of that beauty. But, more I feel akin to the old town's devious, uneven ways when night folds them in a dark, still atmosphere of obscurity. When the eye can see little, the heart takes over.

Then the meandering byways and I come to a quiet understanding. The people who live in shadowy adobes along the way take on a new meaning as night washes time away into oblivion and the past and the present become one. Then the far distant merges with the close at hand and thought knows no boundaries.

By day the encircling mountains are pyramids and prisms of ever-changing color flowing from a substantial base. By night they lose themselves in illimitable space and become neighbors of the stars. Oddly enough, it is then that one really knows these heights where the winds shout and clouds come to a standstill. It is then, too, that one knows each minute pattern of fern and whim of flower petal. It is then that one hears the flutes and bassoons of forest orchestras a hundred miles away.

Tenorio Flat, by day a place quite obvious in the sunlight, becomes by night a stage for the silent actors of the mind. Glancing in uncurtained windows, one will see unruly-haired *muchachos* picking at battered guitars. The Vigil family, with sundry neighbors, will be gathered about an oilcloth-covered table, eating tortillas and beans. Mrs. Apodaca will be bent over her big loom, battening bright yarns to form the thunderbird in a crimson pillow top.

Ignoring the scattered illumination of square windows, one will see at night, not grubby little boys picking at broken guitars, but youth reaching out for songs and cadences. The Vigil family with their friends will not be gathered about a creased and worn oilcloth, but neighbor sharing meager fare with neighbor. It will not be Mrs. Apodaca bending over her bright yarns, but age-old skills and traditions taking form again in one of its countless expressions.

One late winter evening, I went to a gathering in a studio about a mile from my *casita*. When I left, the weather was warm and springlike. When, about midnight we emerged from the warm-curtained studio, we discovered that our high-altitude region had played another prank. From eight to ten inches of snow had fallen. A crooked finger of moon and innocent, big-eyed stars looked down on the heaviest snowfall of the season.

In spite of thin clothing and slippers, I wanted to get into the midst of that pristine world wrapped in night. Avoiding the disapproving warnings of my friends, I started out along an obliterated path I know to the dirt road that skirts the acequia. My feet knew every rock and pitfall of the way. Here, by a fire-hollowed apple tree, was the incline that was slippery as soap. There, by the corner of a wall, would be the pile of adobe bricks that could mean a fall.

Over the road that follows the windings of the old Spanish water ditch, the big cottonwoods met in a shining arch. The soft, wet snow clung to their branches and formed a white tunnel through which I walked. Never in the most remote mountain and desert places have I felt so removed from the world. Although each step sank deep in soft, clinging snow, I begrudged each movement that carried me through the unearthly white tunnel shimmering in the starlight.

When I turned into my own street, I discovered that no one had passed that way since the prankish snow had fallen. My own deeply-indented tracks were the only trace of a human being. I was in a white, untouched world of my own. Reluctantly I turned into my *placita*. With all the soft snow clinging to their walls the little adobes looked like ridiculous square-cut igloos.

In warm bathrobe and slippers, I built a roaring fire of piñón wood and lighted all the candles in the house. This was no night to waste in sleep. Fortified by a yellow pitcher of hot chocolate for myself and a bowl of warm milk for Hijo de Koshare, who had been out in the white night himself, we spent the remainder of the hours until daylight in companionable contemplation. I found myself wondering if Hijo was thinking about other little furry animals tucked away in hiding places in snowy forests.

Perhaps even now the great pumas were stalking about their white domain leaving footprints as I had left mine down my own street. It has been said that Indians think with the heart and not the head. Only on a night like this, could a white person do this.

Snow in Adobe Land

ALL THREE peoples of us in northern New Mexico are united in a love of our *tierra*. To some of us, it is a kind of madness. We love its beauty and the rhythm of its four distinct seasons, no one of which is given to excess or monotony. Even winter here is welcomed.

Snow in our region has a whimsical, an unreal quality. It is not serene and calmly beautiful as it is elsewhere. It seems to know that its whiteness does not belong in a land where all the dye-pots of the world have spilled their colors. It steals in without warning on furtive slipper-tips. It cuts capers. Then it is gone. Only a shrill falsetto of elfin laughter floats down from wind-swept mountain passes.

Yesterday the sky was deepest turquoise and without a cloud. Adobe walls soaked up a mild winter sunshine. Now, this morning, like the soap-writing of prankish boys, there is snow all over everything. Anywhere else in the world, one would say: "How beautiful!" and quote from one of the minor poets. Here the jaw sags open and one exclaims: "Snow!" in about the same tone one would say: "Pixies!"

Snow takes impish liberty with four-square, respectable little adobe houses. It crams a white dunce cap down over scandalized flat roofs. It heaps a frothy meringue on top of substantial adobe walls. It traces a cynical, uplifted eyebrow over a sedate *portal.*

Out in the Indian pueblos, the bronzed children of the sun look like aliens in their own land. To see a Taos Indian, wrapped in his Arablike mantle, stalking through a sagebrush-and-cactus desert disguised with snow, is a ludicrous sight. Even his austere, tip-tilted mesas are ornamented with the soft, ephemeral stuff. He takes one incredulous look and retreats underground to the depths of the kiva, there to practice the intricate steps of ceremonial dances or the song-poems of the ancients. He goes with joy because, in this semi-arid land, snow means moisture.

Some of the Spanish-Americans go to the

opposite extreme. They do not seek shelter underground. Rather they take to their housetops. From here and there over Tenorio Flat comes the rasping scraping of snow shovels. Oddly enough, the shovels are operating on roof-tops, not on paths. Snow on dry, sun-burned *tierra* is one of nature's blessings. Why disturb it? But, on more or less fragile flat roofs, it may be serious business. Only a patient, laughter-loving people would continue to build, century after century, flat-roofed houses at seven thousand feet elevation on the outer fringe of the Rockies.

Much of the male population of Tenorio Flat is on its housetops. Soft Spanish vowels fly back and forth. *"Buenos días,"* greets Mr. Apodaca, like a round-eyed squirrel from behind his chimney. "Where are you going, Señora, in all the snow?"

"To the Plaza to find a roofing man."

Mr. Apodaca, who has one of his children's red-knitted caps pulled down to his eyebrows, and who is twice his natural size in several layers of clothing, gasps with sympathy. "Not that good, fifteen-year-guarantee roof, Señora!"

"No, no—not the roof. It's the *canales,* the little *canales*—gutters. They are solid with ice. Now that the snow is melting, the water can't get through. It's soaking back along the *vigas* and ruining my beautiful white walls."

Mr. Apodaca doubles up with laughter. A roofing man for frozen-solid *canales!* "I'll be over and fix them for you," he offers backing down the ladder. "It will take but a *momento.*"

In a little while he appears with a big brown paper bag and scatters over the solidly frozen *canales* a white, crystalline substance. I have no faith in his kind ministrations. Haven't I poured the contents of a steaming kettle of hot water over the icebergs without results?

An hour goes by and I hear a faint drip, drip from the *canales*. In another hour, snow water is pouring in a steady trickle from the once adamant wooden gutters. My beautiful white walls are saved.

I run back to Tenorio Flat. Mr. Apodaca is nowhere in sight. Piñón smoke is pouring out of dozens of fat chimneys. Geraniums are blooming in old lard pails in every window. "Rahdios" are going full blast.

"Enter, enter," invites Mrs. Apodaca to my knock. "Carmencita, fry the Señora a *tortilla*. A bowl of chile beans would taste good this cold morning. Armendita, put the chile kettle on to heat."

In spite of all the hospitable fluttering, I manage to inquire for Mr. Apodaca.

"The *papá?* Oh, he went to his job with the gas company. Only two hours late and all this snow!"

"He opened my *canales* and saved my nice white walls. Those *canales* were frozen solid—like rocks. I wanted to thank him and find out what he used."

"*La sal,*" explained Mrs. Apodaca, grinding furiously on an imaginary ice-cream freezer. "It's slow, but *poco á poco,* it works."

"Ice-cream salt! Of course," I mutter.

As I struggle home through paths that only the sun will clear, I think of the simple way my Spanish-American neighbors meet the problems of living. A need and something simple to meet that need! And the grace of a buoyant patience, "*poco á poco!*"

Those
Christmas Windows

NOT FAR
from Tenorio Flat there is a place where five
roads meet. They do not meet circumspectly at
accurate angles, but capriciously as if intrigued
with their whimsical irregularity. It is at this
point that I always feel I have reached home, on
my late afternoon return from the Plaza.

This sense of home is always most profound
on winter nights, when darkness covers the sky
and snow the ground. Here the fragrance of
burning piñón wood floats like a veil; and all
the windows in little adobe houses stretch out
golden fingers of light and beckon, "Come in,
come in."

These lighted windows are a kind of calendar of Christmas. Early in December, all the
Señoras are out ankledeep in snow, washing and
polishing the small window panes. Then cur-

tains with big purple and green roses hang like boards stiff with starch and cold, on frozen clotheslines.

All year these deep-set windows are a display-case for family treasures and geranium plants. But, when December comes around, one by one, they blossom like posies in a Christmas bouquet. On such nights, I watch carefully for the evidence of the season.

"Ah," I say at last, "Mrs. Escudero is first again," and I stop to admire. There are the red paper star and the geraniums blooming big and red. How does she manage to time their flowering so exactly? There are the glass candlesticks and two much-worn woolly sheep, with Pablo's bedraggled Teddy bear forming the barnyard scene.

One by one, the Christmas windows of Tenorio Flat blossom and cheer my homeward way. Mrs. Gurulé is given to chains of red and green paper and a huge pottery deer, with a red ribbon around his neck. Mrs. Vigil repeats her usual motif of gigantic cotton snowflakes, strung on thread, and vases full of homemade pink and red tissue-paper roses. Then I see a single candle burning in the Meléndez window, far back in the meanderings of the Flat. That is the window I have been waiting for.

The Meléndez *casita* is one of the poorest in the neighborhood. It is always overflowing with *muchachos,* elderly relatives, and out-of-work *compadres.* Mrs. Meléndez does not have time to string cotton snowflakes nor to contrive tissue-paper roses big as cabbages.

But sometime, years ago before the Five and Dime and crepe paper and red stars and tinsel bells had been thought of, some Meléndez ancestor sat down with pieces of soft pine wood and his knife. He carved out funny fat little sheep and oxen and lop-eared *burritos.* He made a rough little manger. He made his dear familiars, the saints. And, because the saints were great in his eyes, he made them tall so that they look like giants beside the beasts of the field. With natural dyes from the yellow chamisa blossom and the purple flowering bee plant he painted them. Mrs. Meléndez places all the figures in the green forest of her geranium plants. Some of the saints are taller than the forest. Somehow, from Guadalupe Day to the Day of the Three Kings, she manages to have a single candle burning behind the cracked window panes. There I stand and stand, looking at the "beeg, beeg" saints.

But Mrs. Apodaca's window did not bloom as usual among the first. Night after night I looked for it. At last I tapped on her door and asked if they were to have no Christmas window. "It's that Carmencita," she said, shaking her head in a bewildered way. "Carmencita has learned that a rich Anglo lady has offered a prize of fifty dollars for the finest Christmas window in this part of town. Carmencita is working hard to win it. You will hear more later, Señora."

Within a few days, I received a white card printed in Carmencita's vigorous capitals.

"You are invited to see the unveiling of Miss Carmencita Apodaca's Christmas window the night of December twentieth at nine P.M." I sighed, thinking there would be no gentle blooming of a Christmas window here. There must be a dramatic flourish.

At the appointed hour, all of Tenorio Flat stood in the snow before the covered window. A group of *muchachos,* trained for the occasion, burst into what was thought to be appropriate song—"Home on the Range" and "Jingle Bells." Then young Mr. Abeyta and Carmencita pulled aside the concealing blanket and the masterpiece appeared in all its glory. A masterpiece it was!

Out of whitewashed cardboard, they had contrived a little adobe room with ceiling beams of cedar twigs. From one of the beams hung *la piñata,* a small clay jar filled with tiny gifts. Dolls from every household had been re-dressed and leaned against the walls of the room. One of them wore a blindfold and held a small wooden wand, preparatory to hitting the jar to break it. The people of Tenorio Flat stood in speechless admiration and then broke into excited chattering. Nothing like that window had ever been seen before. Old ladies kissed both Carmencita and young Mr. Abeyta.

What was my surprise to hear that the judges appointed by the rich Anglo lady had given the prize to the Meléndez window. Carmencita, I knew, would recover and be off on fresh enterprise; but her poor mother! When I met Mrs. Apodaca, she was all joy and smiling eyes. "They gave Carmencita the Mention of Honor," she said. "Do you think, Señora, Christmas windows should be made for prizes? Christmas windows should grow from the heart. *Verdad!*"

Bilingual Bewilderment

MANY OF US in northern New Mexico speak, to some degree at least, both Spanish and English. This interchange of words has its complications. *Sí* is a little word heard dozens of times a day and signifying yes. It took me many years to learn that it did not mean "yes" according to English-speaking standards. If I meet Roberto, the neighborhood handy man along the road and ask him to come on a certain day to replace a broken window glass, he smiles, looks me straight in the eye and agrees with an emphatic, "*Sí, sí,* Señora." It is very reassuring.

The only difficulty is that Roberto does not appear at the specified time or any other time. The pane of glass and the can of putty I have bought, stand unused and the winds of winter blow fiercely through the broken window pane.

After many such experiences with other Spanish-American workmen, I take my bewilderment to Mrs. Apodaca. "Oh, Roberto," muses my neighbor calmly, "he now has fine steady job working at the Capitol Building. He makes the handy jobs for the *Políticos.*"

"But he said '*Sí*' when I asked him," I protest.

"*Naturalmente,*" nods Mrs. Apodaca, "how else could he make the politeness?"

As nearly as I can interpret her meaning, "*Sí*" means Roberto would like very much to keep the wintry blasts from blowing through the Little Adobe House, but unhappily he is otherwise occupied. Many times, "*Sí, sí*" can mean "No, no," all in the interests of politeness, I am learning.

Then there is the pronunciation of the Spanish letter V. Usually it is pronounced B. As many Spanish-Americans are interested in politics, for many years I was bewildered by ardent references to "boating day" in this arid land, only to find that it had nothing to do with non-existent lakes and ponds, but with the elective franchise.

Ceiling beams in little adobe houses are called "*vigas,*" usually pronounced "*beegas.*"

Great is the confusion of visiting Anglos, because for some unknown reason they substitute an E for the I and call them *begas*. An experienced journalist visited the Little Adobe House to write about it for his Eastern paper. As he wanted local color, he asked the Spanish names for various parts of the house. Notebook in hand, he carefully took down *fogón* for fireplace and *"viga"* for ceiling beam.

"Be careful of that one," I cautioned. "If you are like nine out of ten Anglos, you will spell it with an E instead of an I."

I saw him underlining this important distinction. But when he sent me a copy of his story, right on the front page of his paper, what was my horror to read that the low ceiling of my Little Adobe House was upheld by cinnamon-brown *vegas*—meadows!

My Spanish-American neighbors, when using English, have a bewildering habit of omitting final consonants. I have become accustomed to Spanish-American children blithely caroling, "Home, Home on the Rain."

But Mrs. Pomposo Archuleta's omission of final consonants does not recall poetic concepts. In fact, it recalls the only serious disagreement I have ever had with my Spanish-American neighbors. Mrs. Archuleta and her husband keep the woodyard which has supplied me with piñón wood all the years I have lived here. She always answers the telephone with "Mrs. Pomposo Archuleta's woo yar." I have often wondered just what connection Mr. Archuleta had with the thriving small business. Sometimes I wondered if there were a Mr. Archuleta at all or if he were some kind of mythical figure dwelling among the fragrant stacks of piñón.

This year I found out that there was a Mr. Archuleta. I have even talked with him over the telephone. Alas, we have had words together—meaning that the conversation was not pleasant.

As this has been an unusually mild winter in Santa Fe, when I ordered my second half "tone" of piñón wood, I asked Mrs. Archuleta to send me fine wood. *"Sí, sí,"* she agreed, "I send you fine woo."

But when the wood arrived, it was in great chunks suitable for a winter of continued zero weather. I accepted that load, but when I ordered the next, I begged Mrs. Archuleta to see personally that the wood was fine. *"Sí, sí,"* agreed Mrs. Archuleta, with a note of perplexity in her voice. Again a load of enormous chunks arrived and was unloaded in my garage when I was absent. Otherwise I should have returned it.

When the time came for a third load, I insisted on talking with the ghostly Pomposo himself. He was conjured from some secret hiding place known only to him in the "woo yar," and he answered my call pleasantly and in good English. I reminded him that I had been one of his best customers for many years. I must have fine wood.

To all of which Mr. Archuleta agreed politely. That load also was dumped in my garage during my absence. Alas! it was in even bigger chunks than the other. When I called Mr. Archuleta again from his hiding place, he was emphatic—unpleasantly so. "You ask me for fine woo, Señora, and I send you fine woo. If my woo is not fine enough for you, better try some other woo yar." Then he hung up on me with a bang.

Mrs. Apodaca listened to my troubles calmly and answered from the discreet corner of her shawl held over her mouth. "Fine wood, fine wood," she giggled, "good wood, wood that burn long time. That is what they sent you. Why not say what you mean, Señora: leetle, one half tone of leetle wood."

Sweet
Singing Land

FOR ALL
its gashed arroyos and sculptured buttes, the
high mesaland of northern New Mexico is a
country that flows. It moves in a visible rhythm.
Dye-filled valleys flow against golden hills. Hills
beat in ordered waves against iridescent mountains. Mountains arch and spill into the sky.
Color suffuses color, and shape merges with
shape.

Oddly enough, it is also a land of horizontal
lines, of ruler-straight mesa-tops and four-square
little adobe houses. These act as anchors and
bastions. Otherwise, the entire landscape would
whisk off into space like some wind-driven magic
carpet.

The effect of rhythmed flowing is to make
this a singing land. The ear hears not only the
usual song of storm and wind and the tinkle of

leaf against leaf, but it hears the song of color. Red chiles sing against brown walls. Yellow chamisa sings along dusty roads. Even the wings of raucous *piñoneros* sing of their sky fashioning.

With all their world singing around them, the people here sing, too. Men and boys going to work of a morning sing or whistle as they pass through my yard. Children sing at the drop of a hat. When the *muchachos* come decorously to call, almost their first question is: "Would you like us to sing for you?" Then they burst into song—Spanish song, English song. They are tunefully bi-lingual.

Even the old adobe *maestro* when he comes to "whitewash me," hums and sings as he swings his dripping brush. Once he discovered a guitar hanging on the wall. Without so much as a word he dashed outside, washed his hands under the tap, dried them on his big red handkerchief and settled down for a half hour's contented strumming. In the corner made by my adobe workshop under the silver maple trees, the children of Tenorio Flat gather on summer evenings and sing as long as their *mamacitas* will let them. In the dense shadow of the low-hanging maples, the children are well hidden.

People in the neighborhood wonder where that singing originates. It floats into open windows as if it had no human origin at all.

It is natural for people to sing in this land, where to mention the names of villages is to articulate rhyme and meter.

> Glorieta, Pojuaque,
> Ildefonso, Cochití
> San Antonito, Cundiyó
> Santo Domingo, Chimayó.

I believe our thin telephone directory could be sung without much re-arrangement, so melodious are the names listed:

> Candelario, Aragón,
> Desederio D. Luján.

No wonder that out in the Navaho country, the magic word, "Sing" speeds from isolated hogan to hogan. From miles away they come, on horseback and in covered wagons. Navahos will travel far to buy Navaho songs they do not know. They collect songs as some Anglos collect luster ware.

The Pueblo Indians have been singing since long before written history began, songs of the sun and the sky and the saving rains. The most poignant part of every Indian ceremonial dance is not the rhythm of dancing feet and the beauty of ancient costumes, but the singing of a little group of chanters.

They cluster about the resounding drums and bob gently like feathers moved by an atmosphere of sound. With serious faces they sing the songs of their ancients. In clear tones their monosyllabic words pour out endlessy, weighted with fervor and power.

As they sing, their arms and hands keep up a ceaseless pantomime. The hands say that clouds are gathering over the mountains, the lightning flashes, the green corn rustles with delight. Almost, one is tempted to open an umbrella.

Once, still under the spell of such singing, we left Zía Pueblo on its rainbow mesa-top and started home through the blue-shadowed wasteland. Along the dusty road we picked up an Indian who wanted a ride to Santa Fe. He was a middle-aged, silent fellow dressed in ranchman's clothes topped by a broad-brimmed hat. His hair was cut in the white man's fashion. Evidently an Indian of parts and modern tendencies!

For a long while he sat silent on the front seat. He, too, seemed to be reliving the afternoon's beauties and memories. But as the deep blues of approaching night seeped over arroyo and mesa, the Indian began to sing softly to himself. It was as if he were the only person in all that far-flung empty countryside. Soon his hands were acting out the song in rapid picture language. At last, conscious of an audience, he began to explain, in excellent English, the Indian words he was singing. "The corn, the corn as far as the eye can see," he translated. And we saw green corn waving in that night-filled wasteland. Then he said: "Someone else sing now."

There was someone else in the car who could sing. Her deep velvet contralto rolled out over that fantastic land in "Oh, Susanna," a song Anglos had brought into the country when covered wagons rolled westward over the Santa Fe Trail.

"That is a good song," commented the Indian. "You sing it good, too—the way we try to sing." Then he started his own songs again. Soon the contralto was joining in the old Indian songs, catching melody and words. Wrapped in the songs of an ancient culture sung by an Indian and a white woman, we rolled into Santa Fe. And the land, that far-flung mellow land, sang with them.

Old Songs and New Inventions

INDIANS
are still singing the old songs that started when
the world was young. In time of persecution
they took these songs and sacred chants underground into the depths of the *kiva* and into hidden recesses of the heart. From the red rocks of
Zuñi to the sacred grove of Taos, old songs still
persist. They of all the rich Indian heritage
have been the least touched by modern times.

Manuel Archuleta is a young Indian from
San Juan Pueblo, not far from Santa Fe. As a
boy he was fascinated by the ancient songs and
chants of his people. He could never hear
enough of them. He wandered from pueblo to
pueblo at times of ceremonial dancing and
drank in the highly poetic words and expressive
rhythms of the old chants. But year by year some
of the old songs were gone. Old men who knew

them disappeared and with them went the words and rhythms only they knew.

Manuel is a modern Indian with two years at the University of New Mexico. Then he found work with the Indian Office in Albuquerque. In the same office worked the Indian maiden who was to become his wife. Her Indian name means White Flower and she is from the Pueblo of Laguna.

In the course of events, Manuel made several trips to Laguna to persuade reluctant parents to allow their daughter to marry out of the pueblo. Manuel liked Laguna. He says it is a happy place with the Indians laughing and singing as they go about their work. By a happy coincidence, the father of White Flower was one of the best chanters of Laguna. He not only sang, but he composed many new songs for special occasions. At eighty-five he is still singing the old songs and composing new ones.

When Manuel and his White Flower had married and had a baby to support, Manuel saw an advertisement for a recording machine. Immediately he knew he must have that machine. He would save the songs of his people. Some way, out of his depression-days salary of fifty dollars a month, he made a down payment on that recording machine and tied himself up for additional payments of thirty dollars a month. His family literally lived on fifty cents a day. But he had taken the first step toward his dream.

The next step was no easier. That was to persuade the pueblo authorities to allow their sacred songs to be recorded. Nor was it easy to get the Indian singers and chanters to sing for the modern machine. Many a time Manuel traveled long miles, loaded the singers into a car, brought them to his house in Albuquerque, fed them, and returned them to their pueblo. It was slow, hard work.

The Indian attitude is different now. The governor of Zuñi asked Manuel to come out to Zuñi and make recordings of some of their ancient songs. Indian chanters in groups and solitary singers search out Manuel and ask him to make recordings of their songs and chants.

The original recording machine bought by "going hungry" has been replaced by the latest of appliances. As a sideline to his regular employment, Manuel is building up in his home a small business founded on his recordings. He calls it Tom-Tom Studios. The business is a family affair with his wife handling the commercial end and his three little girls learning.

Although he has never advertised, Tom-Tom records of Indian music are finding their way to music lovers all over this country and in Europe. He is particularly happy over the records that went to India. But the most heart-warming development is that Indians, themselves, almost mob him to hear their own songs played back to them.

When he visits his own San Juan Pueblo, half a dozen Indians grab him and beg him to play his records for them. As San Juan has electricity, many of the Indians have bought record players and Manuel goes from house to house with his growing supply of recordings.

If a pueblo does not have electricity, someone produces the old kind of record player that turns with a crank and the feast is on.

The pueblo dwellers naturally like to hear the recordings of their own songs, but the repertoire now includes Navaho, Hopi, and Zuñi songs as well as those from the Rio Grande pueblos. So has the dream of a young Indian boy been fulfilled to add its part to an intangible fourth dimension.

Acequias Are Open Now

ON THE outskirts of Santa Fe is a vague, indeterminate section known as "the dirt road district." Here narrow roads, yawning with chuck-holes, meander lazily toward uncertain destinations as if there were no such concepts as straight lines and accurate angles.

Along these sunny, dusty roads live many of Santa Fe's writers and artists. Along these roads live also many Spanish-American families, cheek by jowl with the etcher's studio and the poet's tower. And the heart and the keynote of this district is the *Acequia Madre*.

Stiff Anglo tongues learn with much effort and self-consciousness to pronounce *Acequia Madre* with correct attention to soft Spanish vowels and labial consonants. After all the effort and all the practice, it is disconcerting to find that the Spanish-Americans have made a speedier approach to English and refer laconically to "tha deech." That is exactly what the *Acequia Madre* is, the Mother Ditch.

From the early Spanish colonial times, the *Acequia Madre* has carried water to adobe-walled gardens and orchards. It has been here so long that it is more like a natural stream than like a man-made ditch. Tall cottonwoods shade it and fill the air with the silver fluff of their blossoming. Grass makes a parkway on either side where pussy willows bloom in March and evening primroses and mallows are bordered by natural hedges of wild roses. Here grosbeaks refresh themselves after their long spring journey; here clouds of bluebirds, wearing the *azul* of New Mexican sky, settle briefly on crumbling adobe walls.

The Mother Ditch has many children. Small branches wander off from the main stream in all directions. Fortunate is the man whose adobe soil comes within the radius of their wanderings. "Ditch rights" are entered on impressive legal documents.

It is a gala day in Tenorio Flat when the water is turned into its tiny *"contra acequia."*

Mr. Apodaca stays home from his job with the gas company to direct the water on his few hills of corn and fewer chile plants. Mrs. Apodaca, dragging her long black skirts and swathed in her shawl, parades like a gloomy drill sergeant up and down the regimented rows of her hollyhocks. The *muchachos* roll up their blue jeans and wade the little stream with as much shrieking as if it were the broadest of oceans.

Santa Fe is not the only place in New Mexico where there are flowing *acequias*. Each little adobe village in the region has its own Mother Ditch. Around this ditch center the democratic principles of the village, and have since colonial times. A ditch boss is duly elected by the property owners. He can call out every man in the village to help clean out the *acequia* and its tributaries. Each man responds to an emergency like springtime floods, as if it were a call to arms. On that meandering stream depends the life of the village—corn for *tortillas,* chile for sauces *picantes,* and the rich, red-speckled beans.

In every pueblo the Indians are celebrating the opening of the *acequias* with ancient ceremonies and dances to the spring and the quickening earth. In Acomita, the farming home of the Indians who once all lived atop the barren rock of Ácoma, there is excited activity.

Acequias flow full to the brim. Wild plum trees burst into fragile lace against pink cliffs. Little boys on horseback dash wildly about on urgent errands. Men, their heads bound with gay *bandas,* plod up and down the moist, black fields. Women, white-booted and bright-shawled, plaster their rosy homes with deft slappings of pink mud into storm-worn cracks and crevices. There is the contented monotone of singing; shrieks from children falling in and out of placidly-flowing water. The piñón jay with feathers *azules* spreads his wings and demands: *"Piñónes! Piñónes!"*

In what once was called the Great American Desert, three peoples of us, side by side, are stirring in unison to the common verities of soil and seed. There is the promise of fruit tree buds along dark branches. Cloud shadows dapple the sides of distant mountains. There is the musical whispering of flowing water in an arid land. The *acequias* are open.

The Laughter of Genoveva

FOR MANY years now, Tenorio Flat has chimed with the laughter of Genoveva Gutiérrez. Women of Mrs. Apodaca's age and village-rearing do not quite approve. They smother their own laughter under a small brown hand and a hurried: "Excuse it, please, Señora." But laughter rolls from Genoveva as naturally as water sings in little ditches or the meadow lark lifts his ascending notes.

For all its piped water and electricity, Genoveva's adobe is one of the least attractive in the Flat. Her husband has never found time to plaster the adobe bricks on the outside and they are fast raveling away. Many of the window-panes are held together with adhesive tape and the screen door hangs on one hinge. The yard is filled with the broken toys of many *muchachos* and whatever else seems at the time to take up too much room in the small, overcrowded house. Overhead is an entanglement of clotheslines always ballooning with washing.

But, close to the kitchen door, morning-glories and marigolds bloom in summer and always her front window shows side curtains of red velveteen and an ever-changing display of objects of art, including a huge pottery frog, a glass slipper, and a framed picture of Genoveva in her wedding finery. She holds, as was the custom, at that time, a bouquet of flowers and ferns to which her family and friends had pinned dollar bills.

Each year Genoveva and the *muchachos* take in all the joys of fiesta. She puts the sitting-up baby and the lying-down baby in the sagging, creaking go-cart. The two next in years support their uncertain steps by hanging to the handle. Behind come the older ones under their own power, with the two family dogs restrained for the occasion by leashes of twine. Genoveva does not see anything heroic in propelling a heavily laden go-cart with two strap-hangers, the mile and a quarter to the plaza. She has made herself and the little girls flamboyant skirts of fiesta print and the boys have ten-gallon hats made of pasteboard and wear red-and-orange neckerchiefs. She sits along the curb, and her laughter points up the shining armor of parading *Conquistadores* and paces the bugle notes in marching bands.

One indecisive spring day, Genoveva's laughter trilled all morning through the Flat. I could hear the other Señoras chattering and laughing with her. As I peeked curiously around the corner, Genoveva ran to meet me. "Come see what my husban' give me for our *aniversario*. You will never guess. It is a spinner-rinse, Señora. Come and see."

In the center of the tiny kitchen stood a washing machine, all gleaming porcelain and mechanical efficiency. It was even then spinning and rinsing at a great rate. The size of the big oilcloth-covered table had been reduced by half to make room for the spinner-rinse. It looked as if the family would have to eat in relays from now on. Between the stove and the table and the washing machine, there was no room left at all.

Soon new entanglements of clothesline went up overhead in the yard and the *muchachos* played in wildly moving shadows formed by blowing sheets and dresses. It seemed Genoveva must be washing every day in the week and all day. "No, Señora," she explained, "I can do such big washings with the spinner-rinse that now I wash but two days a week. But there is Consuelo Carrillo who has no piped water and more *muchachos* than I have. Naturally I asked her to use the spinner-rinse. Likewise, Señora Pacheco, who has many years and has to draw the water from a well. And many of the women of the Flat wash for Anglo ladies. It seemed only right that the spinner-rinse should do theirs."

I never went to the plaza after that without hearing the noble machine spinning and rinsing in a frenzy of cleanliness. In the shade of adobe walls, women of Tenorio Flat sit at ease, crocheting cotton lace, making paper flowers or chattering while an Anglo machine works for them. Their *muchachos* play under drying clothes blowing in a firmament of clotheslines. One of the poorest adobes in the neighborhood has become a community house and Genoveva a philanthropist of the first water.

It was Mr. Emerson who pointed out that love should make joy, but that our philanthropy is unhappy; that so often we pain ourselves and please no one.

But Genoveva's philanthropy has brought

joy. All the Señoras of Tenorio Flat are gayer than I have ever seen them. Even Mrs. Apodaca sometimes forgets to smother her laughter with a small brown hand. Perhaps laughter like Genoveva's should be an ingredient of all our philanthropy.

However, that Carmencita always passed the hard-working spinner-rinse and the relaxed Señoras with something closely resembling irony in her glance. At last she confided in me. "Just wait," she hissed, "until the Señor of Genoveva gets his water and electricity bills!"

Indigenous

IN A SUMMER
of unprecedented heat and dryness in northern
New Mexico, I look with renewed delight at my
Spanish-American neighbors. From long ac-
quaintance they know more of this lovely unpredictable land than we Anglos. They and the
nearby Pueblo Indians maintain an unper-
turbed gentle harmony with the hot, dry world
about them.

Years ago, when I first came to live in the
Little Adobe House, I consulted with Mrs.
Apodaca as to the advisability of planting a small
lawn in the vicinity of the wild plum tree. Mrs.
Apodaca pursed her lips, gazed upward in pro-
found thought for what seemed endless minutes.

"*Sí,*" she agreed tolerantly. "Is pretty, the
green grass. But this is not green grass country,
Señora—only in high-up mountain meadows."
She looked toward golden hills, light-flooded
mesa-tops and heat-shimmering atmosphere.

137

Then she smiled sadly around the edge of her shawl at the strange intricacies of the Anglo mind. "Lots of work, lots of water so that leetle patch of grass grow beeg. And not so much as one good goat to eat that grass," she groaned, wringing small brown hands at such sophistry.

Mrs. Apodaca's people sweep their yards. In time, the hard-packed *tierra* takes on a rosy patina that reflects in delightful geometric patterns the protruding ends of pine tree ceiling beams, the sturdy bulk of thick walls, and the not too exact angles of roof-line and corners. They look something like the patterns often found on exquisite bowls fashioned by Indian potters. Ever this land repeats in line and color its related designs—horizontal line of sunlight, of straight-edged mesa, of square little houses; turquoise of sky, of front doors, of window trim, pellets dangling from Navaho ears, of flash of wing of the piñón jay.

When *acequias* show not a trickle of water and even piped water is meagerly rationed in Santa Fe, then the indigenous both in flowers and people take on a new importance. Flowers like stock, sweet peas and delphinium look the uncomfortable aliens they are, without their customary pampering by hose and sprinkler.

But the indigenous *rosa de castilla* spreads its green foliage early in spring and follows with such a blaze of little golden roses as I have never seen in rain-nurtured years. It sends out sturdy runners in all directions. It takes over whole garden plots and spills its yellow light like innumerable small suns. It not only lives; it lives exuberantly.

Then come the hollyhocks. They spring up in the strangest places—between flagstones, in the graveled driveway. Straight and confident, like seasoned soldiers, they march through my sun-baked yard and fill the whole place with a rainbow of colors.

In most of the Spanish-American settlements, buckets rattle down into wells and come up slopping water. Anglos, who, at great expense, have installed sprinkling systems they cannot use long enough to do much good, listen to that sound of slopping water buckets with longing and amazement. A new game of treasure-hunting starts all over Santa Fe. Cousin Canuto with a red hollyhock blossom filling a hole in his big hat, has become a person of importance.

"Four Anglos came to me this week," says Cousin Canuto, trying to keep the edge of pride out of his voice. " 'Canuto,' they say, 'can you remember where the well used to be on the place I bought from old Señor Meléndez? Think hard, Canuto; there must have been a well!' They are desperate men, Señora, with hundreds of dollars laid out in trees and plants.

"Of course, Señora, there was a well. It's not so many years ago that our town had no water pipes at all. Often I can remember where the old well was. Then the poor Anglos get out their shovels and dig. Like moles, they dig wherever I tell them. You should hear their whoops of delight when they find an old well that was carefully boarded-over when the fine water pipes reached their property. It is better than a gold mine, Señora."

All over town Anglos have brought in machinery to deepen the old, once-discarded wells. The thump-thump of drilling machinery is heard on the quiet air of Santa Fe. Then an electric pump is installed and the lawns and sweet-peas get all the water they require.

"Want a run of water from my well," asks a neighbor. But from now on I'm sticking to *rosas de castilla* and all the hollyhocks I can encourage. The indigenous has become dear to me. Not only the indigenous of flowers and

140

shrubs, but of thick-walled *casitas* that shut out the heat and of people who walk serenely and confidently in the midst of an uncertain and fickle physical world.

Sometimes I become a little weary with the discussions of erudite Anglos of the region. They are forever fretting whether New Mexico's two indigenous peoples—the Spanish-American and the Indian—will become absorbed by the more energetic Anglos or keep some slight vestige of their native individuality. This summer of heat and drought has taught me the answer to their unhappy cogitations. The unessential will change, but the deep realities will remain like water in the boarded-over, forgotten wells. We Anglos will tap them with our mechanical skill and our ceaseless activity. But it is the same old water that lies buried deep in our *tierra*.

Land of a
Fourth Dimension

WHENEVER
my companion and I explore new roads in northern New Mexico, or retrace old familiar ones,
we always exclaim in unison: "How beautiful!"
Then, after a long silence: "What is it?"

We are trying to discover what makes this
region we love grow increasingly dear as season
follows season in orderly progression. Beauty it
has in endless variety of color and shadow, of
line and mass. But we have each seen many
other regions and lands flooded with color and
formed in breath-taking contours. They all have
their own two-dimensional loveliness.

It is the history back of our region, we
finally decide, that gives it the third dimension
of depth. We know something of that history
which reads like a romance. In all our wander-

ings we are conscious of it. What a pageantry of races, peoples, and events!

We hear the pad-pad of Indian feet through dim mountain passes, along the fabulous Turquoise Trail and up and down the storied Rio Grande. We see the shimmer of sunlight on Spanish armor and hear the hoofbeats of their silver-shod steeds. We hear the cry from windblown hilltops, *"Las caravanas, las caravanas!"* And we thrill to the roar of covered wagons down the Santa Fe Trail. Then we have to acknowledge that, if we knew the history of other regions half so well as we know our own, they, too, would take on this third dimension.

Through many years, the question teased us. "What is it? Why, out of all the world, do we love this region? What does it give us besides the length and breadth of beauty and the depth of past events?"

Then one day, we knew. This land has a kind of fourth dimension which is as intangible and as heart-warming as sunlight. It is a promise of things to come.

Here, in northern New Mexico, we have a glimmer, a whisper of what all the world is seeking in tumult and in sorrow. Here, in northern New Mexico, three distinct peoples are living side by side and evolving a common way of life whose weft is individual and whose warp is common to all. In spite of knotted and broken threads, the pattern still goes on. That pattern did not come through learned commissions nor planned propaganda, but as naturally as the wild plum blossoms along meandering water ditches or aspen gold flows down the sides of purple autumn mountains. It is the result of giving and receiving, flowing between diverse peoples—the dark, earth-wise Indian, the *tierra*-loving Spanish villager, and the westward-moving American of North European heritage.

The first white man—the Spanish explorer and settler—in this region found numerous city-states up and down the Rio Grande. Their inhabitants had built high-tiered homes of the ruddy soil; they grew corn, had devised a system of irrigation, wove vegetable fibers, made exquisite pottery. They had a religion, a government, and a social life which fully met their needs—and which, to a large extent, still do.

For the Spanish settler tossed out in this fantastic land of butte and mesa, of desert and impenetrable mountains, it was dig in or die. He dug in. He was hundreds of perilous desert miles from his nearest base of supply in Old

Mexico. To him came no white-sailed galleons from Spain as came to the relief of other Spanish colonists in Florida, in Mexico and in California.

Along with the settler followed their domestic animals—cattle, horses, and sheep. These the Indian had never seen. In time the colonists brought fruit trees and new edible plants.

In spite of conflicts, giving and receiving —shelter, food, and clothing—flowed back and forth between the two races. No one proclaimed a "Be Kind To Indians Week" or an "Eat More Chile Peppers Week." Commodities and skills flowed back and forth because they were inherently desirable.

Years later, new white men, pushing westward from sparse settlements along the Atlantic coast, found their way through uncharted mountains and finally roared down the Santa Fe Trail. They, in turn, received something of what the Indian and Spanish settler had evolved in the way of shelter, food, and clothing. Significantly, some of them to this day cling to a modified version of all three. They brought with them the tradition of the little red schoolhouse, work— lifted to the nth degree of virtue—and the consuming desire to "make it pay." In time, they contributed machinery and technical skills and pushed back the horizon with ever-increasing transportation.

But it is in the intangibles that this giving and receiving between peoples has attained its greatest import. It is evident in the blending of arts, folkways, and crafts; in the tempo of living; in richness of outlook; in a distinctive grace of living which is the product of us all.

Pattern Named Runaway

THE DOOR
of Mrs. Apodaca's weaving room stood wide
open to summer sunshine and the fragrance of
a blossoming locust tree. She sang contentedly
to herself as her shuttle moved without hurry.

Carmencita, mounted on her bicycle,
passed the door. She sped away, brown legs
pedaling furiously, long black pigtail flying out
behind. Mrs. Apodaca shook her head and
sighed: "She hurries, *pobrecita,* to the U Esse
Post Office to see if she has won in the contest
of the soap people. Her answer was in poetry.
The prize is in cash money. If she wins, she will
buy a brass horn so she can play in the school
band."

A house finch practiced a reedy quatrain
in the locust tree. Water gurgled in the little
"deetch." Next door Mrs. Vigil pat-patted her

day's supply of *tortillas.* If Carmencita got that horn and practiced assiduously, as she would, what would become of all these gentle sounds?

Mrs. Apodaca's shuttle guided a line of soft rose against four lines of creamy tan. *"Poco á poco*—little by little," said Mrs. Apodaca. "Did you ever think, Señora, how patterns run away with themselves? This one started out to be stripe against stripe, the reds and blues the *turistas* like. But after the first few threads, the cliffs of Abiquiú in the Valley of the Cousins came to mind. You know how they are, Señora, pale rose, rosy tan, yellow that looks pink. I had to dye some of the wool myself to get those colors. Mees Boggers has bought it before it is half finished. Sometimes it is good when a pattern runs away with itself."

All day I kept thinking what I could do to save us all from Carmencita's brass horn. She would get one even if she did not win the soap contest. She would peddle Chimayó fruit and chiles from door to door. She would polish silver and wash party dishes. Even the smallest of brass horns—say, a bugle—did not seem fitting for the daughter of a guitar-and-fiddle-playing people.

Poco á poco a pattern began to form that I

might lead Carmencita gently from the brass horn. A concert was to be given for children, a concert of stringed instruments and of wood winds. I bought a ticket for Carmencita and saw her long pigtail hanging over the back of the front row of seats. I chuckled to see her straight little back stiffen with attention when the wood winds went into action. All through the concert, I toyed pleasantly with the thought that a flute might be the answer to Carmencita's musical yearnings.

The next time I went over to Mrs. Apodaca's weaving room, two blond little girls were playing outside the big window. "They are the *muchachas* of the forest ranger," explained Mrs. Apodaca. "In the winter, they live in Santa Fe. I work sometimes for their *mamá*. Carmencita often baby-sits them. They are Anglos *muy, muy, simpáticos.* The *muchachas* brought me a letter from their *mamá,* but I must wait until Carmencita returns from the U Esse Post Office to read it to me. Perhaps you, Señora—"

"The letter says," I skimmed the Señora Forest Ranger's precise backhand, "that they are moving back to the ranger's station in the high mountains in a few days. They would like to take Carmencita along to look after the two little girls. They will pay her fifteen dollars a week and buy her suitable clothes for the mountains. If Carmencita can go, she is to return with the little girls and be measured for her new dresses."

Mrs. Apodaca returned calmly to her weaving. After a few minutes, she remarked: "It's nice place the ranger's station. We make picnic there once. Mr. Forest Ranger played his flute for us."

In a few days, Carmencita came over to show her fine denims. Soft blue they were with pockets and collar of chile red. On her feet were sturdy shoes with what she pointed out as "air-float soles." I told her about the deer she would see night and morning, coming down to drink in the mountain stream. I told her that often I had seen wild animals stand listening quietly to soft music. "Perhaps the forest ranger will teach you to play the flute, so you can play for the deer and their spotted fawns." The pattern was weaving smoothly according to plan.

Soon the ranger's station wagon drove up to collect Carmencita and her baggage. Just before they left, I claimed the ranger's attention. "Carmencita has a great longing to play *música*," I explained. "Do you suppose you could teach her a little about playing the flute?"

The ranger looked pleased. "Sure thing," he grinned. "I even have the first flute I ever owned. It will do for her to start with. In no time at all, we'll be giving flute duets under the pine trees."

Carmencita's intense little face was a shimmer of shining eyes and smiling lips. She put an eager hand on the ranger's sleeve. "Do you think, if I work hard and learn to play the flute, someday I can play the bassoon?"

Time in
Tenorio Flat

MRS. APODACA
has not been her usual serene self. At first I
thought it was because too many big-hatted and
be-shawled relatives had driven in the long, cold
miles from Chimayó. They all had to be fed
mounds of red beans and other viands.

Mrs. Apodaca seemed to have a Spanish
version of Anglo jitters. She was always hurrying. She never stopped for a little chat. She
even refused to work a single day for Mees Boggers. Worst of all, she seemed to be out of sorts
with Carmencita and her flute playing. Another
thing bothered me. Mr. Apodaca seemed to be
cutting wood at strange hours, even late at night.
Could it be that he was going to open a "woo
yar" and do all the woo cutting at night?

At last I went over to *Casita* Apodaca to
find out what had happened. It was only mid-

afternoon, but my neighbor was out in the yard giving the chickens their evening meal. At my uplifted eyebrows, she exclaimed: "Three hours ahead on that job, Señora."

I followed her into the house, taking my usual place on the edge of the old iron bed that had been painted bright orchid for the holidays. Mrs. Apodaca did not come to sit beside me. "Excuse it, Señora," she said absently and started to pound chile paste as if she were pounding her own exasperations.

"I thought you had chile paste on hand for some time ahead," I ventured, stunned by such unprecedented activity.

"*Sí*, Señora, I have some; but this will put me two weeks ahead of what I need."

Then my ears caught a new sound in the room and my eyes strayed to a shelf in the corner. I nearly jumped from my seat on the orchid-colored bed. If I had found a fire engine in Mrs. Apodaca's house, I could not have been more dumbfounded. A cheap, shining alarm clock with an immense bell on top was ticking stridently in the once-quiet room.

Mrs. Apodaca stopped her chile pounding long enough to follow my outraged glance. "*Sí*, a clock, Señora. Carmencita gave it to me. Ever since it has molested me. Teek, teek, teek, day and night that clock goes snipping off time. Señora, if you snip off time into *un millón de* teeks, there is no time left. All I can do is hurry, hurry, and try to get ahead of it."

Time in Tenorio Flat has seldom been measured by "teeking" clocks. At certain intervals there are regular flights of school children coming and going, laborers starting and returning from work, movie-goers headed for the plaza, and their return punctuated by laughter and singing. By these movements, we have approximate notion of time. Sun, shadows, and the very color of our adobe walls fill in the gaps.

My thoughts were interrupted by a little boy who stuck his head in the door. *"Mamacita* wants to know *qué hora es."*

"Is three o'clock," Mrs. Apodaca answered sharply. "Never an hour of the day, Señora, but someone is here asking what hour it is. How did they know before Carmencita gave me that clock?"

"It does tick loud," I comforted. "At home I have an old felt typewriter pad. I'll bring it over and, if you put it under the clock, it won't sound so loud."

"I pour a lot of oil in that clock," Mrs.

Apodaca confessed. "It did not teek at all then. Carmencita took it down town and had it cleaned. It cost two dollars and seventy-five cents. She was quite sad about it. Then that clock teeked louder than ever."

"We may get used to the teek," groaned Mrs. Apodaca, "but that alarm—never in a *millón de años*. Carmencita sets the alarm every night and it goes off the next morning as if the whole town was on fire."

"What time does it go off?"

"At six, the time we have been getting up ever since I can remember. But Carmencita says that alarm clocks are what have made the Anglos a great and rich people."

"Right now I am two weeks ahead on my chile paste, two weeks ahead on my *tortillas,* and three hours ahead on feeding the chickens. The *papá* is a whole winter ahead on his wood cutting. Señora, I have a feeling that, if we get so far ahead of ourselves, we'll pass each other, all going in the wrong direction. As far as I can see, we are not any richer or greater."

The door popped open again and Cousin Canuto inquired in a high childish voice: "*¿Qué hora es?*" and sank, shaking with laughter, into a chair. He took something from an inner pocket.

It was a cheap little wrist watch. "For Carmencita," he said. "It does not have an alarm. Time should be a matter of great privacy." Then he picked up the alarm clock and wrapped it in his red handkerchief as if it were some kind of odious worm.

"What are you going to do with my alarm clock?" demanded Mrs. Apodaca.

"Take it up to my *placita* and bury it among the hollyhocks. Maybe they will blossom a month early."

"Tell me," I asked, "what did the early Spanish settlers do about time?"

"Not a thing," chuckled Cousin Canuto. "You see, they knew that time revolved on an endless spindle. You couldn't get ahead of it, because it was without beginning or end. That is why, Señora, we are still here—and in our right minds."

"Passed by Here"

MANY PEOPLE, viewing northern New Mexico from speeding train or hastening car, think they are looking at a raw, new land. But we who live here, know it is an old land where men of many races and treasures have passed. The valley of the Rio Grande is one of the most historic trails in the world. Countless feet still echo along our dusty ways, and wisps of forgotten songs—Indian, Spanish, French, and English—still whisper in mesa breezes and fill piney valleys with their cadences.

Even the birds recognize the old trails. Persons, wise in bird lore, say that a greater variety of birds pass through New Mexico than through any other state in the Union. Here, not a dozen miles from Santa Fe, I have watched the wild turkey winging from tree to tree. In the high mountains, the arctic ptarmigan blends his white feathers with eternal snows. Early in the spring, wanderers of tropical plumage pause briefly among the wild-rose bushes that line our little "deetches."

Folsom man left artifacts, dating from the end of the last glacial period, in what is now eastern New Mexico. Quite recently, Sandia man, who probably antedates Folsom man by thousands of years, was discovered in a cave not far from modern Albuquerque.

The Indians have a literal way of referring to their prehistoric ancestors, whose ruined dwelling places blend with yellow hillsides and cling to overhanging cliffs. "The People Who Are Gone," they call them. Besides their many-storied homes, their water ditches, and turquoise beads, The People Who Are Gone left many a pictograph on smooth rocks scattered over the New Mexican landscape.

But it remained for a Spanish wanderer to put into words the spirit of this crossroads of the world. On a two-hundred-foot-high wall of red sandstone, he carved with the point of a dagger, his name, the date (1605) and the cryptic Spanish: *Pasó por aquí*—passed by here.

Indian runners, in days gone by, padded

tirelessly over these trails carrying their sky-blue turquoise stones to the kingdom of Montezuma in Old Mexico. They padded back with parrot feathers and shells from a tropical shore to use in their ceremonial dances. Up the valley of the Rio Grande came little bands of Spanish explorers, their metal casques gleaming in the sun and their banners snapping in sage-scented breezes. Following them came Spanish colonists, their pack animals and squeaking *carretas* loaded with meager equipment. Through dark canyons beyond Taos penetrated fur-capped mountain men from Kentucky and the French provinces.

White covered wagons crossed a prairie sea to find a safe harbor in old Santa Fe. The Butterfield stage roared into old Mesilla. The pony express, carrying Lincoln's latest message, broke the stillness of the desert night.

Prehistoric red men, Navaho, Apache, and Pueblo Indians, Spaniards, Frenchmen, and Anglo-Saxons passed by here. They passed and left their names on ruddy cliffs, pictographs in hidden caves, a bit of turquoise jewelry, the hilt of a Spanish sword, a fur cap and a long musket, and the ballads of the world.

Something less tangible, but vastly more important has remained. From the long processions of men who "passed by here" has come a certain unself-conscious tolerance for all kinds of men. It has not come about through learned societies or mass propaganda. It is a natural mellowing in an old, old land.

One wintry day, when our little Plaza looked like a mica-decorated Christmas card and narrow San Francisco Street was almost obscured with wind-driven snow, the aged governor of a nearby Indian pueblo stood under the *portal* of one of the stores.

The old man stood alone, taking in the sights of town with alert, twinkling eyes. From his bulk one would guess that he wore several pairs of trousers and many shirts and coats against the cold. His long, flowing white hair was bound with a purple *banda*. On his hands were elegant, brown kid gloves and crooked over one arm was a little bamboo cane, such as boys buy and carry at country fairs. Evidently the old Indian had done his best to make his attire worthy of an infrequent trip to the state capital. His creased bronze face held strength and a great serenity.

White men, bent against the gale, recognized the old governor and stopped their hasty steps to shake hands and welcome him. Bits of conversation reached my eavesdropping ears. "Was there any danger of floods when spring came? When did they expect to open the *acequias?* The Green Corn Dance! Sure he'd be there. Hadn't missed it for twenty years."

It was just one man of the soil greeting another and asking questions that seemed important to them both. One was a white official in a local bank and the other was the venerable governor of a red man's adobe world.

Along came two little Spanish-American urchins, carrying between them a tall, steaming pail of tamales for sale. And a good day it was for their merchandise! They went into a huddle, then opened the pail and offered the old governor a hot, steaming tamale.

Deliberately he rested his bamboo cane against the building and peeled off his fine kid gloves. Then he ate three tamales in unhurried succession, much as if they were bananas. When he had finished, he reached into an inner pocket for coins to pay the *muchachos.* But they shook their heads, picked up their steaming pail, and disappeared in the flying snow.

No set of rules and regulations on race relations could have produced that little drama on the stage of San Francisco Street. I seemed to hear the pad of many feet coming down the snowy crossroad, and the wind was singing old songs in many tongues along the frozen river.

One Little
Indian Girl

NEW WAYS
take strange forms with young Indians just as
they do with young Spanish-Americans. To me,
the effect of this age on the youngsters of an
older way of living is endlessly exciting. Why
not observe it at close range in the Little Adobe
House?

Therefore, I let it be known, through various Indian grapevines, that an employed Indian
girl could have free room in exchange for small
services around the periphery of her working
hours. Perecita appeared in answer to the grape-
vine broadcast. She had finished as much school
as she thought necessary and had obtained work
as a clerk in a chain store to which she gave
full title, even to the "Incorporated." Her home
was in one of the most conservative of the Rio
Grande pueblos. In her full, bright skirt and

puffed-sleeve, off-the-shoulder white blouse, she was a delight to the eyes.

I gave her a key to her detached adobe house under the silver maple trees and a key to my own front door. The next day she appeared calmly asking to borrow my keys. "What happened to yours?" I questioned.

"Well," explained Perecita in a matter-of-fact way, "I go to the movies at night with my girl friend, María. I have no purse, but she have purse. So I ask her to put my keys in her purse. She do. Then she go home to her pueblo with my keys."

"And what is María's pueblo?"

"San Juan," answered Perecita unconcerned.

"But San Juan is a modern pueblo and not far away. Drop María a card and ask her to put the keys in a little box and mail them to you."

"I cannot and she cannot," said Perecita with finality.

Weeks later, she came in with a letter in her hand. "You remember María, my girl friend, and the keys? She could not mail them to me until now. She has been in prison."

"In prison!"

"Yes, she get home from movies with me

late and her mother in San Juan sent her to her grandmother in Picurís, way back in the mountains. So, at last, she is out of prison and back in San Juan. I get the keys today." Perecita giggled and I chuckled with delight. Evidently Indian mothers in modern pueblos maintain discipline.

Time was a concept my little Indian grasped but vaguely. Some mornings, she appeared in my kitchen to prepare her breakfast twenty minutes before she was due in the store a mile away. She hummed contentedly as she prepared eggs and toast. Other mornings, she would awaken me before sunrise. "Couldn't you decide on a breakfast hour somewhere between mid-morning and the crack of dawn?" I inquired, somewhat perturbed.

"How can I?" asked Perecita, who evidently had no watch.

"I'll put an alarm clock in your room tomorrow."

Perecita looked at me and grinned. "Already have good alarm clock," she giggled, rubbing her stomach.

In time I had almost a secretary's job taking my little Indian's telephone calls. Many of them were from another Indian who said her name was Twinkle. It seemed Perecita had borrowed Twinkle's silver *concha* belt and she wished its immediate return. The reason for her insistence, she explained, was that she was leaving Santa Fe with her "Dad and Mom" to visit relatives far away. Try as hard as I might, I could not imagine Indian parents accepting the titles of "Dad and Mom."

From all I could gather my little Indian was not selling very much in the "Incorporated" store. Soon she was working but two or three days a week as a clerk, and completing her budget by day work in the neighborhood. Her worldly possessions were increasing with each dollar she earned—and in one direction only. They were aids to beauty—jars and boxes of creams and powders, hair-washing mixtures and hair-curling apparatus. One night I observed her headed for her room with what appeared to be sticking plasters all over the smooth bronze of her young face.

"What in the world happened?" I gasped.

"Wrinkles," sighed Perecita heroically, laughing with her skin strained in a dozen directions under the plasters.

But even with these drastic aids toward the white man's standards of beauty, Perecita evidently was not much of a salesperson. At last, the manager of the "Incorporated" store told her she would have to leave. She tried many other stores in town, but stores, too, have their grapevines. Perecita was reduced to day work in the neighborhood.

One day her mother appeared at the door of the Little Adobe House. She was in full pueblo regalia, with such turquoise and silver jewelry displayed on her person as would drive a collector mad with envy. As she spoke no English, our conversation had to be conducted in Cousin Canuto's Language of the Heart. If I had only been able to play the *guitarra,* I am sure we would have done better.

Perecita showed her all over the place. "My mother say to tell you she like your house," the daughter interpreted. "She say it is beautiful. She say it looks just like her own. It makes her homesick. She is catching next bus for home." And that I shall always consider the highest compliment my little adobe has ever received.

After a long conference in Perecita's room, they returned. "I go back to pueblo," said my little Indian. "If I start doing day work, I can do it all my life. Next fall I go back to school and learn more so I can earn living like white girl.

Then I come back and stay with you again." For the first time, there was a catch in her voice.

Only one newly-acquired luxury Perecita left in her room. It was a little box of sticking plasters—for the wrinkles.

The Rhythm
Of Jémez

NOVEMBER twelfth usually finds me in the Jémez Indian Pueblo, watching the Harvest Dance. Each year the pink-walled settlement seems more beautiful and dearer to my heart. There is a rhythm there beyond the pat of hundreds of dancing feet, beyond the booming rawhide drums, beyond the cadenced voices of the chanters. There is a rhythm of color—pink houses cheek by jowl around the sanded plaza—a backdrop of high, rosy cliffs and a blue mountain topped with snow.

But there is also a deeper rhythm of peace and well-being. Fat animals look placidly out from wattled corrals. Flat roofs hold long ears of corn—purple, blue, orange, and red—stacked up like firewood to dry. The children are plump, well clothed, and as playful as kittens.

There is friendliness everywhere—smiles, the wave of a hand. But, in spite of all the years, I had been in the little pink-walled houses only to buy Indian corn and strands of chile peppers. Did the rhythm I felt outside permeate the interior of their homes? Was it a part of family and friendly living? For years I did not know.

Then there was another question. How did children, mere babies, learn all the intricate steps? How could they take part in the ceremonial with such solemnity and precision? Exact replicas of their dancing elders they were—hand-woven kilts, abalone shell at the neck, blue spruce twigs at elbow and knee, and deerskin moccasins with twinkling silver buttons.

The answer to these two questions came in due time. A friend had placed a large order for pottery which the women potters of Jémez were to make. She had placed the order through a young Jémez Indian who was employed in Santa Fe, but who kept his home and family in the old pueblo and spent only his week ends there. Did Amado feel that his children could have a better rearing in their Indian environment? Did he still want to keep his own roots in the ancient pink soil of Jémez? He was young, well educated, and income-producing. What was holding him to the little settlement in the shadow of the blue mountain?

Night was falling when we returned to Jémez. It was a Jémez we had never seen before. No drums were pounding in the plaza. No hordes of visiting Navahos were wandering about, jingling silver jewelry. No white spectators were patting Indian children on the head or talking broken English to their elders.

This was a place where people lived their everyday lives. Smoke from supper fires drifted lazily upward. Men moved without hurry, to feed the animals in their wattled corrals. Women with pails in hand gathered at public water-taps. Children brought in armloads of juniper wood. Jémez became, for the first time to me, a home town with real people in it.

Amado was waiting for us on the steps of his smooth-plastered little house. Around him three or four children were playing. He was dressed in ordinary workingman's clothes. But, when he introduced his wife, we saw that she was wearing pueblo feminine finery—deerskin boots with silver buttons, a back mantle of bright silk, edged with lace. She was as casual and at home in her beautiful costume as we were in our heavy skirts and sweaters.

171

Inside, the little house was almost all one big room. There were two big beds against the wall and a table under a window where the pottery was spread out for inspection. A beautiful corner fireplace sang with flames. There was something clean and uncluttered about the place that rested the eye.

From some back room, Amado brought four old-fashioned dining room chairs and placed them side by side in an exact row down the center of the room. There we sat somewhat stiffly, while neighbors and potters came in, were introduced, and shook hands with the surprising limp handclasp of the Indian. Our vigorous hand-shaking seems a breach of good manners to them.

My three companions soon went over to look at the pottery on the table. But I could not move because I had spotted in the firelighted room an old Indian sitting on the edge of the farther bed. He was holding a nine- or ten-months-old baby on his knee and beside him was a small ceremonial drum. The old Indian was in overalls and denim jacket, but a red silk *banda* held back his long grey locks. He held the baby with one hand and a rattle gourd with the other.

Just as if no one were in the room, he

was putting that big-eyed infant through the rhythms of Indian dancing. He rattled the gourd gently and moved his knees and arm as if he were dancing. Sometimes he thumped out a few notes on the drum beside him. Then the baby would crow with delight and move his fat arms and legs in exact tempo. At such times, the old Indian's face shone with a radiance that did not come from blazing logs. It was an inner light. Then our eyes would meet in an understanding that passed all the barriers of races and faiths.

As we were leaving, "Come back," urged Amado. "When you come out to a dance, come to our house. Come when there isn't a dance."

Neighbors and potters waved their hands. The old Indian waved his rattle gourd with one hand and the rhythmic baby with the other. I could not bear to leave this night-filled, tranquil Jémez, with the big stars close to flat roofs and the glow from fires turning windows into squares of light.

Adobe Madonna

LUPE padded heavily over to the homemade blue crib in a corner by the whitewashed fireplace. She was like that heavy-walled room of hers—sturdy and squat and comfortable. "He sleeps," she thought, her wide, dark face more Indian than Spanish, as impassive as the walls around her. "If he sleeps, I can do what has to be done."

Señora Montoya sat elegantly in the one chair the room afforded. Around her, up and down ranged the beds of a numerous family. The scent of burning wood and drying chiles clung to the air. "Is better for Pepe. No?" Her words rattled against the heavy stillness like hail on the flat roof.

Lupe kept thinking about the charity woman. It was she who had started all the trouble after Santiago had died. "Ten children," she had gasped, staring around her with unbelieving eyes. "How are you going to feed them without a husband? We can't help you forever." She had seemed worried, the charity woman. She had made many trips over mountain roads to their little adobe village. She had fought her way through snow and sliding mud.

One day she had come in wrapped in cheerfulness like a shawl. With her was Señora Montoya, the wife of the storekeeper in the village beyond the purple mesa. "Señora Montoya will take Pepe, the baby, and make him her own son," she had said. "Some day he will be rich. He will have the store and the sheep and the goats. It's just too wonderful," she had added, beaming at Lupe's blank face. "Without a baby, you can work the *ranchito*. And it will be one less mouth to feed."

Everything about the fair-haired charity woman was mysterious to Lupe. She represented the strange authority of the Anglos—an authority that could send a man to jail or make a child go to school when he should be weeding the chile patch. Blank of face, Lupe had signed the papers the charity woman had brought.

Lupe stood looking at the baby in the

bright blue crib, at his cap of black hair like the coat of a little black rabbit, at his skin that was the color of sun-baked adobe, at his straight legs and his chest curved like a wild gourd. Even the charity woman said he was the most beautiful baby in all northern New Mexico. He was not like the motherless Quintana *niño*. *Pobrecito*, with its ugly face and skinny legs.

Lupe lifted the sleeping Pepe in her great arms and placed him in the hollow lap of Señora Montoya. The Señora jingled her gold earrings and pressed the soft weight of the baby against the stylish, silk-covered breast that had never felt the imprint of a child's head.

"Is better for Pepe. No, Lupe?" She kept repeating the words, her eyes avoiding the wide, stolid face of the other woman. The nine older children huddled together in a corner. They were poised like quail ready to scurry in all directions at the first crackle of alarm.

Señora Montoya eyed their ragged overalls, their faded dresses and bare, brown feet. "This little one," she gloated, rocking Pepe in hungry arms, "will not go to school in rags. Nor will he carry a folded *tortilla* to eat when noontime comes. We will send Pepe to the Brothers in Santa Fe when he goes to school. He will have blue corduroy *pantalones* and white shirts and fine brown shoes.''

The nine older children continued to stare at the rich Señora. She was so rich she had had something done to her hair. It was frizzled like the new spring leaves on the cottonwood trees. She carried Pepe away in a car that didn't have to be cranked from the front nor pushed from the rear. They whooped and yelled. Their mother just stood.

Lupe left the empty crib in the corner by the fireplace. Santiago had made it many years ago. Often now, when she was drawing water from the well under the apricot trees, she would think she heard Pepe's thin, outraged wail. She would let the bucket drop back with a splash into the deep water. Running and panting she would dash into the house. Sometimes when she was milking the goats or chopping a log into firewood, she would stop suddenly and make for the house. At sight of the empty crib she would remember and wipe her face with a corner of her skirt.

As she went about planting the corn and the beans, she thought in patterns as heavy as her body. Why had they taken Pepe away? They could have given him goats and blue *pantalones* in his own adobe. They hadn't given the other children so much as new overalls. But the other children were not beautiful like Pepe. She stood stiffened with the idea. They had taken Pepe away because he was beautiful. The charity woman had said that the Ugly One, the *niño* of Simón Quintana, would have to get along as best he could with whatever care the neighbor women might give, until his *papá* found another wife. No one wanted the Ugly One. Already his *papá* was making sheep's eyes at little Albina Hidalgo who had a waist no bigger than an aspen tree.

Hidden by the row of geranium plants in old tin cans, Lupe peered through her deep-set window that night. Simón Quintana hurried by, limbering his middle-aged stride toward the adobe of his young love. Lupe smiled with ancient understanding as she slapped her long black shawl over her head and shoulders. Like another shadow, she disappeared in the night-filled arroyo. Softly she pushed open the door of an adobe that smelled of stale grease and unwashed clothes.

A feeble cry like a night bird's note came from something bundled in an old wooden crate. "Ah-h," she muttered, sniffing clotted milk in a sour feeding bottle. Gently she rubbed the little skinny legs. Round flashing eyes noted filthy clothes and body. "Ah-h, *pobrecito,* little Ugly One," she wept.

Swiftly she wrapped him in the folds of her old black shawl against her breast. Back up the arroyo she strode with a strange feeling of power in every step. It was as if music went ahead of her and gave wings to her feet.

In front of her fireplace she bathed the thin little body. There were a few of Pepe's poor ragged garments left, disdained by the rich Señora Montoya. "Is good the warm goat's milk," she coaxed as she tucked the Ugly One under the flour-sack sheet in the bright blue crib. "Sleep, little *piñonero,*" she sang as she walked up and down the sturdy walled room. Out of regimented beds, end to end along the walls, brown strong arms and legs spread in all directions. Lupe's eyes smiled as she surveyed her brood.

When the charity woman came a week later, Lupe dusted off the one chair for her occupancy. But she, herself, stood like a butte of solid granite.

Suddenly the charity woman's face lost its schooled composure. Baby noises were coming from the bright blue crib that should have been empty.

"Is only the Ugly One, the *niño* of Simón Quintana," Lupe explained. "No one wanted him. No one at all."

The Singing Heart

HIPOLITO
came noiselessly around the corner of the Little
Adobe House into the back yard. Without clatter and without banging, he emptied the waste
can into a tub he would carry back to the truck
which waited on a cross street. On top of the
waste, he placed the lid from the can and started
to walk off with it.

"The lid, Hipólito," I called. "You forgot
to put the lid back on the can." Hipólito smiled
gently, replaced the lid and, without a word,
moved tranquilly on into Mrs. Apodaca's yard.

In a few minutes, he returned. After him,
at some distance, pursued Mrs. Apodaca in unprecedented haste. Her shawl blew out behind
her like a banner as she ran, calling: "Hipólito,
Hipólito, *mi tapa*—lid. *Un momento, Hipólito,
mi tapa.*"

Hipólito smiled gently and presented the
lid to my breathless neighbor, as gracefully as if

it had been heaped with roses. She received it with equal grace and a *millón de gracias.*

"*Ay,*" murmured Mrs. Apodaca, sinking down on a box under the wild plum tree and fanning herself with an end of her shawl, "that Hipólito is *muy, muy preocupado.*" She did not say it with any fault-finding in her voice, but with a certain note of pride. "You see, Señora, Hipólito is *un poeta.* He make the poetry for weddings and fiestas in all the little villages around here. *Naturalmente,* he must be *preocupado.* While he is collecting trash, he is theenking, theenking singing words to say to brides and to make happy the dances. *Sí,* he is *el poeta* for all this part of the country."

But not everyone took Hipólito's *preocupado* condition, with its lid-disappearing propensities, as did Mrs. Apodaca. There were, I heard, some complaints on file in the Department of Sanitation. They originated with Anglos, who had neither covers to their waste cans nor poetry in their hearts.

The situation reached a climax when Mees Boggers' lid disappeared one day, while she was away from home and unable to watch the poetic collector of trash. Unhappily, it was a new lid from a new and shining trash can which had cost

Mees Boggers four dollars and eighty-nine cents
—or so it was reported.

Mees Boggers called the Department of
Sanitation and complained bitterly of the out-
rage. The head of the Department assured her
that the new and costly lid would be recovered
and returned to her without delay. After many
such calls, she was told at last, jubilantly, that
the lid had been retrieved and that Hipólito, in
person, would make a special trip to restore it to
her. Days passed, but no lid!

It was fortunate for Mees Boggers that the
arrival of important friends from her home city
of De-troy-eet diverted her mind from the irrita-
ting situation. The friends, it was reported over
the neighborhood by Mrs. Apodaca, were stopping in our grandest hotel and in the most expensive rooms obtainable.

Immediately these distinguished friends
invited Mees Boggers to luncheon. To keep in
touch with this exciting turn of affairs, Mrs.
Apodaca offered her services in Casita Boggers
which she had long allowed to go dust-filmed
and unswept. *"Sí*, she look like a queen, that
Mees Boggers," reported Mrs. Apodaca, "when
she leave for that 'lonch.' "

"Did she wear her Navaho or her Fiesta

costume?" I asked, feeling it would be one or the other.

"No, no," corrected Mrs. Apodaca with some heat, "she wore a silk suit that whispered when she walked and a blouse as fine as spider's web and a beeg hat with blue and white leelacs around it. She had pink paint on her fingernails and her hair went around and around her head in ripples. On her hands were beautiful white gloves. She did not walk to the plaza, as she always does. She took a cab. She had to, because her slippers had the heels *so* high." Mrs. Apodaca measured off a generous four inches with thumb and forefinger.

I, who have always seen Mees Boggers in regional attire, with Indian moccasins on her feet and a beret pulled firmly down over straight locks, thrilled to the information.

"She came back in the cab, too," continued Mrs. Apodaca, "and beside her on the seat was the leed of her trash can. She seemed a little *histérica*. I ran and brought her a glass of water and then she told me what happened.

"Her friends were waiting for her in the open door of the fine hotel. Just as Mees Boggers came walking toward them on her high heels, with hands in white gloves outstretched, at that *momento,* Señora, up drove Hipólito on his trash truck. For once he was not *preocupado.* 'Mees Boggers, Mees Boggers,' he called so everyone could hear, 'I have eet, the leed to your trash can!' Down he jumped from his truck, ran up the walk and placed the beeg, shining leed in Mees Boggers' hands covered with the beautiful white gloves. She was so upset that all she could do was to stand holding that beeg leed in front of her. Her friends and the *turistas* standing about looked at her with eyebrow lifted. When she could speak, Hipólito had vanished on his truck.

"For a *momento,* I was afraid Mees Boggers would complain about Hipólito and he would lose his good job. But she started to laugh. She laugh till the beeg tears run down her face. 'It could only happen here,' she gasp. 'Even the trash man makes the poetry while he gathers the trash.' "

Mrs. Apodaca peered anxiously out from the folds of her black shawl. "What is so funny about that, Señora? What does it matter what a man does with his hands if he has the singing in his heart?"

Awake in the Sun

MANY erudite sociologists, anthropologists, and other serious-minded people worry unhappily about what they call the "impact" of modern times and Anglo ways on our Indian and Spanish-American neighbors. Will they lose their distinctive ways and customs? Will they be absorbed? One factor I have never heard the intelligentsia mention is that "impact" works both ways. We Anglos, too, are changing with modern ways and with our contact with the distinctive customs and philosophy of living of these neighbors.

The ones who worry the most are some of our regional poets and artists. They cling to the past as drowning men cling to a raft. A couple of them kept talking about a couple of little villages they knew not far from Santa Fe. Even their names, Chupadero and Río en Medio, were beguiling. It seems they slept in the sun of a dreamy valley where wooded hills made dim blue and violet shadows and where a languid stream barely moved. The Poet and the Artist had not been there for a number of years, but they assured me that there would be no change.

"Just pages out of an old Spanish romance," the Poet said, "blown into a hollow of the New Mexican mountains and miraculously preserved through the years."

The Artist described the sun-gilded adobe houses against which pink apricot blossoms hung in spring and scarlet chiles in autumn. The people there were content to follow the lovely drama of seedtime and harvest. Modern living had never touched them. Therefore, they were beautiful.

My friends, the Artist and the Poet, are of the cult which believes that beauty resides only in the past and they clutch it frantically to their hearts. The drama of the region is a tale that is told. They disdain my exuberant contention that the greatest drama of regional history is taking place now in our beautiful, fantastic land. Indians and Spanish-Americans of mature years are looking calmly and critically at this modern age, the product of Anglo activity. Their deliberate selectivity seems a hopeful omen for all races, worthy of the poet's most singing words and the artist's rarest colors.

This selectivity is founded on a sturdy retention of much that has proved good in their past. Both Indians and Spanish-Americans are loyal to their indigenous, thick-walled adobe habitations, which we Anglos try to copy. They keep their skillful ways with seeds. Water ditches still sing their way in a silver network over the russet soil and the fruits of harvest dry in the high, rare air. They keep their faith in the unhurried rhythm of the seasons and of time's comfortable continuity. They still delight in color and their good craftsman fingers know the joy of making things.

It is a wholesome experience to watch these two races sampling the Anglo's contributions to a way of life. With what aplomb do they finger the Anglo's vaunted ways and wares! Some they try and vehemently discard. Some they weave into their own design for living.

I have seen, in a small mountain village, big-hatted men driving their horses and goats around in a circle to thrash out their golden grain. And over the next ridge I have seen a Taos Indian, white-sheeted as a Bedouin, driving the latest thing in tractors over the pueblo communal acres. Hands, now busy with clutch and gear, at night might well be busy with ancient ceremonial properties in the depths of the underground *kiva*.

In spite of electric wires and modern machinery, I notice that María Martínez of San Ildefonso still makes her famous black pottery without the help of the potter's wheel. The Spanish-American weavers of Chimayó still run the shuttle by hand through the warp strung in their simple looms to make their blankets. The silversmiths of Zuñi still tap-tap on their tiny anvils to produce their exquisite silver and turquoise jewelry.

It was a day in early June when the Artist, the Poet, and I finally started for the extolled villages of Chupadero and Río en Medio. I noticed that my friends appeared not in a lovely, horse-drawn wood wagon, but in a somewhat battered Cadillac. As we rolled into the mountains, the Artist began his Cassandra song.

"Take a good look," he warned. "What with Los Alamos just across the valley, this untouched forest of spruce and pine may soon be buried in the depths of the earth. It would take just one good explosion to do it. Centuries later they will dig it up as petrified wood and sell it to the tourists—if there are any tourists."

No one paid any attention to him, because the wild strawberry blossoms were white along the roadside. The spruce trees wore trim blue-green uniforms laced together with silver, and the aspens were tossing out the green confetti of their leaves. In little glades, wild iris made blue and lavender splotches like a child's scribbling with colored crayons.

The Spanish villages were all they had been heralded to be. No one screamed the morning headlines. A boy in a bright blue shirt led his horses down to the stream to drink. Women hung yellow, scarlet, and lavender dresses on lines strung between houses. Big-eyed children peered from behind sheltering walls. All was peace, "quaintness," and beauty.

"You see," gloated the Artist, "just as they have always been. Tomorrow I'm bringing my easels and paints up here."

We went into a little store that was the front room of an old adobe house. A goat slept in one corner. Drying chiles, onions, and corn hung from the ceiling beams. No one came in to buy anything, although I noticed that the shelves were well-stocked with expensive canned foods.

"How many familes live here?" asked the Poet in his best high-school Spanish.

"Sixty-four in Chupadero, sixteen in Río en Medio," the storekeeper answered in English.

"You see," gloated the Poet, "eighty families are making a living from the soil here just as their ancestors did. It must be a good living from the look of things for sale on the shelves. And they are doing it in peace and beauty."

"No, no, Señor," corrected the storekeeper gently. "Nearly all the men work away from here."

"And where do they work?" bristled the Artist.

"In Los Alamos," said the storekeeper.

Old Crossroads of the Nation

NEW FOOTSTEPS are whispering along this old crossroads of the nation which we call New Mexico. As yet it is only a whisper, a shadow, a portent. A locality is like a person. The obvious gives it personality. The hidden and elusive give it individuality. What an individual is the region around Santa Fe!

It basks in the sun and IS. Its roots are sunk in the adobe of one of the world's greatest crossroads. From the footsteps of Sandia man to the outcry of a watcher a-top Atalaya Hill yelling the biggest news of the day, *"Las caravanas, las caravanas!"* it has felt the impact of new races, new peoples, new ways.

The hum of motors along hard boulevards, the flight into blue spaces between the stars, the trail of the atom! Still the region remains as secretive and elusive as the Sphinx. It keeps its tongue in cheek, but takes all trail wanderers into the warm circle of its piñón-freckled arms. There something as timeless and as inevitable as nature's processes has taken place. One evidence is that the essentially masculine and Anglo banker, storekeeper, or cattleman sports in bracelet or ring the sky-blue stone of the Turquoise Trail. The Indian orders a pair of copper-riveted denim overalls, made by union labor, from the mail order house. The boy from an incredible Spanish village, sixty miles from an electric wire, flies a plane for a commercial company above the ruts in the old Santa Fe Trail.

A few years ago when drought threatened the region, its inhabitants went about a remedy, each in his own way. The Archbishop asked supplications before the stone altar piece of Cristo Rey, in the Cathedral that shelters *La Conquistadora* (who knows something about trails), and in all the little adobe churches of the vicinity. The Protestants prayed for rain in the accents of Calvin, Luther, and the Book of Common Prayer. Out in the Indian pueblos, the Indians danced.

It rained. Suddenly and without warning

it rained. The poplars and cottonwoods clapped vociferous castanets. All the acequias sang with water and the Río de Santa Fe ran bank to bank. The whole Dirt Road Section of Santa Fe was ankle deep in mud—wonderful mud.

The Indians came to town shawl-wrapped and deerskin-booted. They practically took over San Francisco Street. They bought fruit and cream puffs by the dozens. They consumed gallons of ice cream. Were they just celebrating? Or did they think their dancing had broken the drought? A lot of Anglos thought it had.

It takes the light, light touch in the old crossroads—such as the little Spanish secretary gave an inquiring voice over the telephone. The caller had noticed an adobe house for sale on the outskirts of town. A battered sign gave the name of some real estate man and his telephone number. The Anglo called the number and asked to talk with the man whose name was on the sign. "No, he is not here," the secretary said in soft Spanish accents. "I am sorry, but you cannot talk with him."

When she was questioned as to when the real estate man might be available, she hesitated. "I do not think he will be back," she said gently. "You see, Señor, he died two years ago."

Even the seasons of the year have a light touch in this old crossroads. Snow is not snow here. It is regional play-acting. If winter here is just an act, spring is sheer whimsey. It comes in horizontal layers of color, spread one above the other. First is the red, wet soil which big-hatted men stir with horse- or burro-drawn plough or which a white-draped Taos Indian turns with the latest in tractors. Above the layer of soil is the layer of fruit-tree bloom, pink of peach and apricot, white stippled with pink of apple. Then follows the dull orange layer of hills and the blue of mountains, with an ever-active sky-sea overhead tossing clouds about like spume.

Days of fruit bloom pass gently into days of jewel-red cherries in the walled, fragrant orchards of Chimayó. Small adobe houses stand in roof-high forests of hollyhocks. Cottonwoods and poplars shake lazy, green feather dusters against the sky. Shadows trickle across a wall that holds a *santo* in a niche. A shower sluices between the mountains. All the wooden *canales* on adobe houses spout miniature waterfalls. Shawl-wrapped Señoras dash out with a red-flowering geranium in an old lard can. A double rainbow bends over a sparkling, pristine land.

Its ends point to new treasures to be found in this region that constantly beckons "something new beyond the ranges."

All the play-acting of winter and the whimsey of spring and the rainbows of summer are but curtain raisers for the region's time of splendor. Then the very atmosphere gives off a sheen. All the little adobe houses and all the high garden walls are gilded and outlined in color like a page in a medieval tome.

Indian farm wagons roll in from the fields, heaped high with corn that repeats every color of the spectrum. Spanish-American women sit around blue wells in hard-packed adobe yards and string chiles red as vigil lights. In canyons, scrub oak spreads a crimson foreground between yellows, repeating the colors of the gay banner of Spain that once floated over the land. But high overhead and out of reach stretches the Indian emblem of the sacred turquoise.

No one knows what new, less tangible trails will meet in this region in the future. Even now may be heard the faint rustle of approaching wanderers. The artists and the poets hear it. The everyday man who has caught a little of the "feel" of the land senses it.

I have seen Los Alamos from a hill above

the village of Río en Medio as night swept down the valley like an obliterating sea. There, little mechanical toys shuttle along highways like so many beetles. A plane cuts the angle of Black Mesa. Then night washes in between the hills. Suddenly, across the valley against the deeper black of huddled mountains, a whole plateau springs into unearthly light. Seemingly a city from another planet, Los Alamos bursts into sudden blooming like some air-sustained flower. But that city of light is upheld by the old, old bulk of the Parjarito Plateau, where trails are worn knee-deep from the feet of "The People Who Are Gone."

Where so many footsteps have passed and mingled, one learns not to take one's own too seriously. Like the calendar of the seasons one acquires the light, light touch. It could not be otherwise in what Mary Austin calls "a land whose beauty takes the breath like pain." Always there is the sense of hearing faintly the voice of some hilltop watcher, "the caravans, the caravans are coming!"